LAW AND WAR OF

OF WAR AND LAW

David Kennedy

PRINCETON UNIVERSITY PRESS

PRINCETON ✚ OXFORD

Library of Congress Cataloging-in-Publication Data

Kennedy, David, 1954–
Of war and law / David Kennedy.
p. cm.
Includes bibliographical references and index.
ISBN-13: 978-0-691-12864-1 (hardcover : alk. paper)
ISBN-10: 0-691-12864-2 (hardcover : alk. paper)
1. War (International law) I. Title.
KZ6396.K46 2006
341.6—dc22   2006012483

British Library Cataloging-in-Publication Data is available

This book has been composed in Adobe Garamond and Myriad

Printed on acid-free paper. ∞
pup.princeton.edu

Printed in the United States of America

3 5 7 9 10 8 6 4

May the human freedom of responsible decision be
the vocation of our politics

CONTENTS

ACKNOWLEDGMENTS

Numerous friends and colleagues have contributed generously to my thinking about war and law, and to this essay. I am particularly grateful to Arnulf Becker, Nathaniel Berman, Dan Danielsen, Charles Dunlop, Tom Franck, Ryan Goodman, Janet Halley, Duncan Kennedy, Paul Kennedy, Martti Koskenneimi, Mike Lewis, Ian Malcolm, Michael Schmitt, Dale Stephens, Detlev Vagts, Glenn Ware, and Ken Watkin for comments on various drafts.

I began this project more than twenty years ago as part of a broader inquiry into the history of international law. The many students and friends who contributed to the various parts of that earlier study have also influenced this book. Let me acknowledge again the hands of Nathaniel Berman, Laurent Cohen-Tanugi, Clare Dalton, Charlie Donahue, Mort Horwitz, Bob Meagher, and Detlev Vagts in my earlier study of sixteenth- and seventeenth-century international legal thought: "Primitive Legal Scholarship," 27 *Harvard International Law Journal* 1 (1986). That study was written under the powerful intellectual influence of my friend and mentor Duncan Kennedy, who has contributed more than anyone to my thinking about law and war and much else over the intervening years. Our common readers will instantly see the impact of Duncan's masterful study "The Rise and Fall of Classical Legal Thought"[1] on this essay as well.

In 1987, I published a second piece of my historical study focusing on the transition from nineteenth- to twentieth-century international law that was marked by the end of the First World War and the establishment of the League of Nations, as "The Move to Institutions," 8 *Cardozo Law Review* 841 (1987). David Charny, Tom Franck, Tim Goslant, Tim Sellers, David Shapiro, Cam Stracher, Dan Tarullo, and Detlev Vagts were tremendously helpful in that endeavor. At the same time, I was working on a study of international legal doctrine, *International Legal Structures* (Nomos, 1987), which took up the broad structure of the contemporary laws of force. Nathaniel Berman's influence can be felt in both works. For twenty-five years, I have thought about international legal modernism and intellectual method in collaboration with Nathaniel, for whose intellectual generosity and friendship I could not be more grateful. Nathaniel's terrific recent study "Privileging Combat? Contemporary Conflict and the Legal Construction of War"[2] should be read by anyone with interest in the themes I raise here. He develops in doctrinal detail a range of themes I only echo here.

I considered the relationship between humanitarian professionalism and the use of military force in the final chapter of an earlier book, *The Dark Sides of Virtue: Reassessing International Humanitarianism* (Princeton, 2004). This expands themes sketched there, rooting them in the history of efforts to place war in a legal framework. Over the months since that book appeared, I have been fortunate to receive reactions from numerous audiences to the arguments about the limits of different humanitarian strategies I developed there. Those conversations and engagements have enriched this book enormously.

From the start of my career, Tom Franck has been a steady friend and intellectual comrade. For me, Tom embodies the highest promises of the international legal imagination, and his thinking on the role of law as a currency of political legitimacy will be visible on every page of this book. I would never have taken my thoughts about warfare out of the classroom had Dale Stephens and Glenn Ware not encouraged me to do so. Their trust and willingness to share their military experiences and perspectives of the 1990s with a conscientious objector from the 1970s made this book possible. I would also like to thank the many participants in the June 22–24, 2005, United States Naval War College conference "The Law of War in the 21st Century: Weaponry and the Use of Force" who made valuable suggestions and comments on the portion of this study I presented there. Viewpoints expressed are, of course, mine alone.

War Today

War is a profound topic—like truth, love, death, or the divine.
Intellectuals from every field have cut their teeth on it: political scientists, historians, ethicists, philosophers, novelists, and
literary critics. But war is not one thing, always and everywhere. People write about the wars of their own time and their
own country.

The wars of my time and my country—the America of the
"postwar" half century—have been varied. We have fought a
cold war, postcolonial wars, and innumerable metaphoric wars
on things like "poverty" and "drugs." Our military has inter-
vened here and there for various humanitarian and strategic
reasons. The current war on terror partakes of all these. When
framed as a clash of civilizations or modes of life—secular and
fundamentalist, Christian and Muslim, modern and primitive—
the war on terror is reminiscent of the Cold War.

Like the Cold War, the war on terror seems greater than the
specific conflicts fought in its name. It transcends the clash of
arms in Iraq or Afghanistan. On their own, those wars resem-
ble postcolonial and anticolonial conflicts from Algeria to
Vietnam. When we link the war in Afghanistan to women's

rights or the war in Iraq to the establishment of democracy, we evoke the history of military deployment for humanitarian ends. In our broader political culture, the phrase "war on terror" echoes the wars on drugs and poverty as the signal of an administration's political energy and focus. At the same time, the technological asymmetries of battling suicide bombers with precision guided missiles and satellite tracking has made this war on terror seem something new—as has the amorphous nature of the enemy: dispersed, loosely coordinated groups of people or individuals imitating one another, spurring each other to action, within the most and the least developed societies alike.

Strictly speaking, of course, terror is a tactic, not an enemy. We use the phrase "war on terror" not only to disparage the tactic, but to condense all these recollections in a single term. By doing so, we situate this struggle in our own recent history of warfare. The phrase also frames the broader project with fear, and marks our larger purpose as that of reason against unreason, principle against passion, the sanity of our commercial present against the irrationality of an imaginary past. In this picture, we defend civilization itself against what came before, what stands outside, and what, if we are not vigilant, may well come after.

It is not novel to frame a war in the rhetoric of distinction— us versus them, good versus evil—nor to evoke a nation's history of warfare each time its soldiers are again deployed. When we call what we are doing "war," we mean to stress its discontinuity from the normal routines of peacetime. War is different. To go to war means that a decision has been taken: the soldier has triumphed over the peacemaker, the sword over the pen, the party of war over the party of peace. Differences among us are now to be set aside, along with the normal budgetary constraints of peacetime. This is serious and important—a time of extraordinary powers and political deference, of sacrifice and national purpose.

The point about war today, however, is that these distinctions have come unglued. War and peace are far more continuous with one another than our rhetorical habits of distinction and our wish that war be truly something different would suggest. A phrase like "the war on terror" can evoke so much precisely because wars of metaphor have blurred with the wars of combat on the ground. The distinction between them is far more tactical assertion than material fact.

This can be easier to see in hindsight. Take the Cold War. It was an enormous military and diplomatic—and economic and ideological—struggle, carried on by the political, military, and commercial elites of both superpowers for more than a generation. At the same time, until the Soviet Union's surprising collapse, it was always plausible to insist that the Cold War had long ago ended, that the many proxy wars and great power interventions we now remember to have taken place in its name each had its own more specific logic, and that the long and stable peace between the blocs was itself frozen, rendering the rhetoric of "Cold War" a somewhat retro political vocabulary for justifying this or that policy priority. In this account, relations between the blocs were governed not by the law of war, but by the stable law of "coexistence."

Was it war—or was it peace? Looking back, as historians, we could argue either way, for surely the Cold War was both a titanic global struggle *and* a period of remarkable stability among the great powers. Throughout the period, however, experts and politicians, citizens and pundits disagreed about which to emphasize. And their disagreements had stakes for policy and politics. Was détente a dramatic "opening," or the belated recognition of an established order among the world's powers? Was the nuclear standoff itself the end of history, at least the history of great power military struggle? Or would that end only come after we had accelerated our spending on arms to a level unsustainable for our adversary? As these questions have become matters for historical interpretation, it is easier to see positions about them arrayed on a spectrum, and to treat those who would argue one *or* the other as straining in a way that seems tendentious or partisan. We feel we can tell something about someone who argues one way rather than the other—something about his or her politics or personality. Distinguishing war from peace is both a serious political decision and a symbol of partisan positioning.

There are parallels in our current "war on terror." Should we have responded to September 11 as an attack—or as a terrible crime? Are the prisoners held at Guantanamo enemy combatants, criminals, or something altogether different? These are partly questions of tactic and strategy, about the appropriate balance between our criminal justice system and our military in the struggle to make the United States secure. Strategic debates about the relative merits of offense—taking the fight to the enemy abroad—and defense here at home are likewise framed by the question of whether this is, in fact, a war we are fighting. But security is a feeling as much as a fact, and these are also questions of political interpretation. We can imagine a spectrum of positions, from insistence that the country remain on a war footing, at home and abroad, to the view that we treat the problem of suicide bombing or terrorist attacks as a routine cost of doing business, a risk to be managed, a crime to be prevented or aggressively prosecuted.

In short, the boundary between war and peace has become something we argue about, as much or more than something we cross. War today is both continuous with—and sharply distinguishable from—peace. As policy, the difference will be one of degree—what *balance* of policing and military action? What balance of offense and defense? But these differences are also matters of ideology and political commitment. War today is both a fact and an argument.

This book follows the threads of these two observations—the increasing continuity between war and peace, on the one hand, and the continued rhetorical assertion of their distinctiveness, on the other—to understand what makes the wars of our time and place unique. Both threads lead to law. It has become routine to observe the omnipresence of law in our peacetime culture. The same has become true for war, and the result has knit war and peace themselves ever closer together. Warfare has become a modern legal institution. At the same time, as law has increasingly become the vocabulary for international politics and diplomacy, it has become the rhetoric through which we debate—and assert—the boundaries of warfare, and insist upon the distinction between war and peace or civilian and combatant. Law has built practical as well as the rhetorical bridges between war and peace, and is the stuff of their connection and differentiation.

To understand—and accept—these continuities between the politics and practices of war and peace, we must understand more clearly what it means to say that warfare has become a legal institution. When we think of war as sharply distinct from peace, it is easy to imagine it also as outside of law. War is often the exception to the routine legal arrangements of peacetime; contracts, for example, routinely exempt acts of war alongside "acts of God." If we pause to think about the law relevant to war, we are likely to focus on international rules designed to limit the incidence of warfare, from the ancient "just war" tradition, to the institutional machinery set in place by the United Nations Charter to "save succeeding generations from the scourge of war." Or the many disarmament treaties limiting the use or availability of the most heinous weapons—exploding bullets, gas, chemical, or nuclear weapons. Or the rules of humanitarian law regulating the treatment of prisoners of war or those wounded on the battlefield. We are likely to think of these rules as coming from "outside" war, limiting and restricting the military. We think of international law as a broadly humanist and civilizing force, standing back from war, judging it as just or unjust, while offering itself as a code of conduct to limit violence on the battlefield. Indeed, it is common to associate this entire legal universe with the International Committee of the Red Cross, itself borrowing something from the neutral and humanitarian image of its Swiss hosts.

But law is relevant to war in many other ways. The military, like other public and private bureaucracies today, operates in war and peace against the background of innumerable local, national, and international rules regulating the use of territory, the mobilization of men, the financing of arms and logistics and the deployment of force. Taken together, these laws can shape the institutional, logistical—even physical—landscape on which military operations occur. Today's military is also itself a complex bureaucracy whose managers discipline their forces and organize their operations with rules. Armies have always been disciplined by rules, usually legal rules. The national regulations by which Nelson disciplined the Royal Navy at Trafalgar were tough, parallel to those of British criminal law of the era. Under the Articles of War, a man could be hanged for mutiny, treason, or desertion. Routine discipline was to be enforced through flogging and "starting," or striking a man across the back with a rope or rattan cane.

The interesting point is that in Nelson's day, these rules were distinct both from contemporaneous international legal debates about the "justice" of warfare and from the rules governing the French and Spanish fleets. In the years since, as the military has become a more complex modern bureaucracy, linked to the nation's commercial life, integrated with civilian and peacetime governmental institutions, and covered by the same national and international media—and as our ideas about law have themselves changed—the rules governing military life have merged with the international laws about war to produce a common legal vocabulary for assessing the legitimacy of war, down to the tactics of particular battles. Was the use of force "necessary" and "proportional" to the military objective—were the civilian deaths truly "collateral?" What is difficult to understand is the extent to which this vocabulary—of just war, legitimate targeting, proportionate violence, and prohibited weaponry—has been internalized by the military. Not every soldier—not every commander—follows the rules. Rules are bent and ignored. Rules are violated. But this is less surprising than the astonishing way the legitimacy of war and battlefield violence has come to be discussed in similar legal terms, by military professionals and outside commentators alike. As such, law today shapes the politics, as well as the practice, of warfare.

In the first chapter of this book, I explore the political context within which this merger of law and war has become significant. The forms war and law assume vary with the nature of politics and statecraft. The legalization of our political culture, and the emergence of a global policy class of experts who respond to the same media and speak the same language, has altered the relationship between war and law. It is only in this context that we can understand what it means that lawyers are increasingly forward deployed with the troops, or that planned targets are routinely pored over by lawyers. This is the context in which it seemed sensible for opponents of the Iraq conflict to frame their opposition in legal terms. The war, they said, was *illegal*. For all his contributions to legal codification, it is hard to imagine Napoleon consulting a lawyer to discuss targeting. In the same way, it would have been bizarre to oppose Hitler's invasions—let alone the Holocaust—principally because they were *illegal*.

The emergence of a powerful legal vocabulary for articulating humanitarian ethics in the context of war is a real achievement of the intervening years. What does it mean, however, to find the humanist vocabulary of international law mobilized by the military as a strategic asset? How should we feel when the military "legally conditions the battlefield" by informing the public that they *are entitled* to kill civilians, or when our political leadership justifies warfare in the language of human rights? We need to remember what it means to say that compliance with international law "legitimates." It means, of course, that killing, maiming, humiliating, wounding people is legally privileged, authorized, permitted, and justified. At the same time, how should the U.S. military itself react to the escalating public demand that it wage war without collateral damage— or to the tendency to hold the military to an ever higher standard as its technological capabilities increase?

The legalization of modern warfare has a history. It is customary to relate changes in modes of warfare to the political history of ideas about sovereignty and the nation, and to changes in the material and technological capacities of the military profession. But the changing nature of warfare is also a function of changing ideas about law. The second chapter of this book explores that story. When law saw *itself* as an autonomous discipline, external to the institutions it regulated, it was more difficult for legal ideas and rules to infiltrate the military professions, or to become the political vocabulary for assessing the legitimacy of strategy and tactic. When the legal profession understood law as a framework of sharp distinctions and formal boundaries, it was easier to think about war and peace as sharply distinguishable legal statuses, separated by a formal "declaration of war."

As late as 1941, it seemed natural for the United States to begin a war with a formal declaration, as Congress did in response to Pearl Harbor. In the lead-up to both world wars, the United States carefully guarded our formal status as a "neutral" nation until war was declared. That Japan attacked the United States without warning—and without *declaring* war—in violation of our neutrality was a popular way of expressing outrage at the surprise attack. In the years since, the formal status of neutrality has eroded. Moreover, when Israel launched a preemptive strike against Iraq's nuclear capability, there was plenty of outrage—but it was not expressed as a failure of warning or declaration. Something had changed. In the late nineteenth century, law provided a set of categories and distinctions whose violation could seem an outrage. These categories persisted thru the middle of the last century, and their vocabulary of distinction is with us still. Meanwhile, however, the broad legitimacy of warfare and military tactics were not evaluated in legal terms prior to the Second World War. A legal institutional process and doctrinal vocabulary for doing so had begun to be developed for that purpose by the start of the twentieth century, but it would only catch on after 1945. As a result, across the twentieth century, the legal experience of war reversed. The categories came to seem far too spongy to be the occasion for outrage, while in a broader sense, warfare had become a legal institution.

Across the twentieth century, more antiformal and flexible ideas about law joined hands with a more professional and bureaucratic idea about warfare to make the interrelationship between law and war more pronounced. And it became far easier to think of war as a matter of "more or less," separated from peace (as belligerents were separated from neutral powers) more by the political claim to be engaged in the serious business of war than by any formal or institutional boundary. These changes had particular significance for efforts to restrain warfare through law. The humanist legal strategy of standing outside the military while insisting upon compliance with external humanitarian standards was joined by efforts to infiltrate the military with bureaucratic legal restrictions. Today's humanitarians blend these two strategies, seeking to restrain war's violence by oscillating between external denunciation and internal partnership with colleagues in the military. In large measure, their strategies have been successful. Military professionals find the same external standards conditioning the political environment within which war is fought, and use the same internal norms of conduct to mobilize and discipline the force. Military and humanitarian professionals are speaking the same legal vocabulary.

All this was in place by the end of the Cold War. Since then, of course, the international order has been dramatically transformed. The emergence of a global economic and commercial order has amplified the role of background legal regulations as the strategic terrain for transnational activities of all sorts, including warfare. Sharp boundaries between the political and institutional cultures of the first, second, and third worlds have dissolved, heightening the significance of the shared legal language of the world's political elites. In the years after the fall of the Berlin Wall, the humanitarian institutions

and professions that call themselves "civil society" quickly became more prominent players on the world stage, heightening
the significance of their humanitarian and human rights vocabulary for global political and legal debate. The legacy of
successful—and decidedly unsuccessful—partnerships between
global humanitarian, diplomatic, and military actors over the
last decade has complicated all of their relationships to an increasingly shared legal vocabulary.

It is not new to observe that at the same time, the nature of
warfare has itself changed. The Second World War—a "total"
war, in which the great powers mobilized vast armies and applied the full industrial and economic resources of their nation
to the defeat and occupation of enemy states—is no longer the
prototype. Experts differ about what is most significant in the
wars that have followed. Our wars are now rarely fought between roughly equivalent nations or coalitions of great industrial powers. They occur more often at the peripheries of the
world system, among foes with wildly different institutional,
economic, and military capacities. The military increasingly
trains for tasks far from conventional combat: local diplomacy, intelligence gathering, humanitarian reconstruction, ur-
ban policing, or managing the routine tasks of local government. It is ever less clear where the war begins and ends—or
which activities are combat, which "peacebuilding." In combat,
enemies are dispersed and decisive engagement is rare. Battle
seems at once intensely local and global in new ways, as informal networks of fellow travelers exploit the financial and com-
munications infrastructures of the global economy to bring
force to bear here and there, or global satellite systems guide
precision munitions from deep in Missouri to the outskirts of
Kabul. Violence itself seems to follow patterns better understood by study of epidemiology or cultural fashion than military

strategy. Taken as a whole, the political, cultural, and diplomatic components of warfare, both globally and within the sphere of battle, have become more salient.

The third chapter of this book explores the significance of war's legalization for these developments. As many in our own military have already well understood, there are new opportunities for creative strategy. They have a term for the waging of war by law—"lawfare."[1] In today's asymmetric wars, moreover, law can be weaponized quite differently by our own technologically sophisticated forces and by the dispersed groups of terrorists and insurgents against whom they have found themselves in combat. At the same time, the legalization of warfare offers new opportunities for those who seek to restrict the use and violence of military force. Millions of people marched against the Iraq war buoyed by the claim that the war was an illegal violation of the UN Charter.

But there are not only opportunities. In the last part of the book, I focus on what can go wrong when humanitarian and military planners share the same legal strategic vocabulary—wrong for humanism, and wrong for warfare. The relatively stable modern legal management of warfare has been put under new stress with the rise of asymmetric modes of warfare. Indeed, the twentieth-century model of war, interstate diplomacy, and international law are all unraveling in the face of low-intensity conflict and the war on terror. Most worryingly, the legalization of warfare has made it difficult to locate a moment of responsible political discretion in the broad process by which humanitarians and military planners together manage modern war.

1 ✛ War as a Legal Institution

The Political Context for War

Nearly two hundred years after he made the observation, Clausewitz remains correct: war is still the continuation of politics by other means. In broader terms, modern war reflects modern political life. In large measure, our modern politics is legal politics: the terms of engagement are legal, and the players are legal institutions, their powers expanded and limited by law. The tools and outputs of the political process are often legal norms; the tactics of political maneuver now moves in an increasingly complex legal process. We are not surprised by the number of politicians—not to mention lobbyists and political professionals—who are lawyers. To say that war is a legal institution is not only to say that war has also become an affair of rules or the military a legal bureaucracy. It is also to say something about the nature of the politics continued by military means.

Looking back, it is easy to see that warfare was altogether different in a political order of independent princes making war with private armies than it would be after the establishment of a Europe-wide order of states mobilizing national armies to defend the national interest. Likewise, when most of the world was governed by a few European colonial powers, warfare was different than it would become after decolonization, when national and international politics everywhere was organized through more or less integrated "nation-states." To understand modern war, we must understand the global—and national—context within which the politics of peace and war are waged.

Although the world's surface remains organized in territorial nation-states, each, at least in name, absolutely sovereign, the international political system today is a far more complex multilevel game than the rows of equivalent national flags arrayed at UN headquarters would suggest. States and their governments differ dramatically in powers, resources, and independence. There is something audacious—and terribly misleading—about calling them all states and respecting their nominal leaders as "sovereign." Even in the most powerful and well-integrated states, moreover, power today lies in the capillaries of social and economic life. Governments are no longer—if they ever were—the only or the predominant political actors. Vast networks of citizens, commercial interests, civil organizations, and public officials determine much of what any government, or any president, is able to say or do.

Moreover, we have become accustomed to the vulnerability of our national economy—and our own jobs—to global economic forces. We understand that our nation is not "sovereign" in any absolute sense when it comes to economic matters. American trade law scholar John Jackson put it this way:

Interdependence may be overused, but it accurately describes our world today. Economic forces flow with great rapidity from one country to the next. Despite all the talk about sovereignty and independence, these concepts can mislead when applied to today's world economy. How "sovereign" is a country with an economy so dependant on trade with other countries that its government cannot readily affect the real domestic interest rate, implement its preferred tax policy, or establish an effective program of incentives for business or talented individuals? Many governments face such constraints today including, increasingly and inevitably, the government of the United States.[1]

The difficulty comes in extending this realization to the world of public policy, and to questions of war and peace.

It is no surprise that national leaders who sought power with domestic legislative agendas find themselves drawn to foreign affairs—and favoring the military and the bully pulpit to advance their agenda. Any president would be tempted to use the media and the military for all manner of projects, and to blur the boundary between "real" and metaphoric war. We only need to remember how road bills were passed and the interstate was built during the early Cold War as an exercise in "national security." Nor is it surprising that presidents should so often use the military and media together. The Cold War was fought commercially and culturally more often than militarily—and by racing to put a man on the moon. The only hot wars and military campaigns—Korea, Vietnam, Nicaragua—were smothered in hostile media attention by the end. It is not surprising that we sent messages with our arms budgets more often than we sent missiles. Or that we got more traction from our music and movies than all our spies and diplomats.

But, of course, no president is able to pull the levers of media and military power alone. To say that the Pentagon reports to the president as commander in chief is a plausible, if oversimplified, description of the organizational chart. But it is not a good description of Washington, D.C. There are the intelligence agencies, the president's own staff, the political consultants and focus groups. Born alone, die alone, perhaps—but sovereigns do not decide alone. The bureaucracies resist, the courts resist, the dead weight of inertia must be overcome. We must remember that half of Washington wakes up every morning to ensure the president does not succeed. Although scholars have long debated the constitutional powers of the president and Congress in matters of war and peace, the Constitution is not a reliable description of the way our political system—or power in our world—is constituted. The decision to make war belongs neither to the president nor to Congress, any more than other policy initiatives spring whole from the political commitments of individual politicians or are the product of disembodied entities we refer to as the "legislature" or the "executive." These decisions are imagined, designed, debated, defended, and adopted by people in an extremely wide range of institutional settings, in the United States and abroad.

Those who share the war power with the president are not the world's citizens. Even the voting citizens of the great military powers participate primarily as an imagined audience for media presentations of government action. Political leaders today act in the shadow of a knowledgeable, demanding, engaged, and institutionally entrenched national and global elite. The people who push and pull on governments are not all statesmen or diplomats or government officials. By and large, they are professionals and experts—lawyers, economists, businessmen, academics, journalists, and the like—who work in a wide range of private and public institutions. These professional elites, at home and abroad, are the political context for war.

As a result, *expert consensus* can and does influence the politics of war—consensus, for example, that Iraq had weapons of mass destruction, that American credibility was on the line, that something must be done, that dominos would surely fall. We now know that although September 11 opened a window of plausibility for the invasion of Iraq, the campaign had already long been under way—and not simply because the leadership, the Bush family, say, was "obsessed" with Iraq, but also, and more importantly, because an entire administrative machine had been set in motion, with its own timetables and credibility requirements. The invasion incubated there, in the background, built momentum through hundreds of small decisions, budgetary, administrative, political, rhetorical, public, and private. In some sense, of course, Bush could have called the whole thing off, and without his enthusiasm all that momentum may never have built. The interesting point, however, is that by the time we focused on "the president deciding," it is not at all clear how much room to maneuver he still had. "The United States" had made a commitment to overthrow Saddam Hussein—a commitment whose political and bureaucratic momentum could not easily have been stopped without incurring all manner of further costs—long before the decision came to the president—let alone the UN Security Council—for explicit decision.

The assessments of background elites are matters of ideological commitment as well as professional judgment. They can be incredibly stable, outlasting one leader after another, like the broad establishment consensus in the United States about the importance and meaning of "containing" the Soviet Union throughout the Cold War period. But elite opinion can also change—sometimes quite rapidly. This can happen when new facts come to light, or simply because some segment of the political class loses heart or finds itself stirred to a new fashionable cause. The rise and fall of consensus among political elites is also a matter of debate and constant formal and informal renegotiation among those elites. Sunday morning television, the op-ed pages of the elite newspapers, conversations in boardrooms and dinner tables all contribute to the negotiation of political aims and limits for war. This was clearly visible in the fallout from the prisoner abuse scandals in the Iraq war. They affected the status of forces among elites debating all manner of broad and narrow issues relating to the conflict and to America's place in the world. Both nationally and internationally, they influenced perceptions of the relative power of the American military and civilian leadership—and of the power of the American "hegemon" more broadly.

Of course, the political context for the use of force is different in every nation. Despite the formal institutional similarity of national governments—they all have foreign ministries, defense ministries, health ministries, just as every American state has a state bird and flower—these institutional forms will only rarely reflect parallel political cultures. This is easy to see where the national state is weak and local warlords control autonomous militia. But it is no less true in nations like Canada where the national political consensus sanctions the use of force primarily for peacekeeping. Or, as in Japan, where the main levers of national power are financial and institutional rather than cultural or military. Or in Brussels, where the European Union has no significant military—or media—lever, but only law and regulation. It is not surprising that Europe would respond to the foreign policy challenges posed by the fall of the Berlin Wall by extending its regulatory regime eastward, arriving in one after another nation with the promise of membership and the thousands of pages of legal "acquis communitaire" through which the regimes of Central and Eastern Europe would be changed. Elites pursue foreign policy agendas—perhaps to change the regimes in their immediate neighborhoods—with the institutional machinery, financial resources, and legal powers they have.

As a result, the global political system is an uneven fabric of quite different, often mal-aligned institutions and players. Across some national boundaries, moreover, the links are dense and deep, across others few and weak. The international regime itself is a fragmented and unsystematic network of institutions, some public, some private, which are only loosely understood or coordinated by national governments. The chatter of diplomats in hotel suites and official meeting rooms animates an extremely specific and limited world. Innumerable national and local constituencies, private actors, corporate and financial institutions, loose transnational networks, and religious and other groups that stretch beyond the national territory are all part of the political context within which war and peace are made.

At the same time, violence has become a tactic for all sorts of players—warlords and drug lords and freelance terrorists and insurgents and religious fanatics and national liberation armies and more. States have lost the monopoly on metaphoric, as well as actual warfare. War is now the continuation of a far more chaotic politics, in a far more chaotic political environment. Violence can be the work—or simply the potential work—of "our" extremists. Al Qaeda, the Taliban, five angry men in London or Bali or Beirut can also continue their politics by military means. The interests expressed through the violence of war are heterogenous and partial. It is not "all about oil" any more than it is all about establishing a new

Caliphate from Grenada to Jakarta. The call for "jihad" lies on the same continuum as declarations of "war" on teenage pregnancy, on communism, or on the government of Saddam Hussein.

Putting all this together, all governments have less focused power to decide for war and peace than they had a century ago. For political scientists, this means that any so-called realism that attends only to the overt acts of national sovereigns is no longer realistic. For military professionals, it means that neither the commander in chief nor the political culture of Washington controls the politics of the battlespace. As often as not, it will be the reverse—the politics of battle determining the political culture of the leadership. For all actors, humanitarian and military, friend and foe, it means the opportunities and sites for political engagement and vulnerability are far more numerous than we are accustomed to imagining. It can be difficult to come to terms with the fact that the common impression of more unilateral presidential authority in foreign affairs is simply not accurate. In a sense, this is completely obvious—but it is difficult to remember. Participants in the policy process, at home and abroad—including the president himself—are prone to forgetting that just because he can act does not mean he can be effective. And, of course, the same is true for the military. Acting is one thing—achieving a desired political result will be a function of the broader political context.

I should be clear that this does not mean, as many commentators have suggested, that *multilateral* rather than unilateral action will always be more effective. The effort to extract normative rules of action—multilateralism is good, unilateralism is bad, say—from sociological observations about the nature of the contemporary political order is not new. But it can be terribly misleading. The international political order is fragmented and chaotic. Political actors are enmeshed in ever more complex webs of reciprocal and asymmetric influence. But this "is" does not translate easily into an "ought." The political context *may* reward multilateral action—but it may not. Sometimes unilateral action will be applauded and followed. The point is that whether the context will reward unilateral or multilateral action *in a particular case* will itself be decided by the largely uncoordinated reactions of hundreds of individual and institutional players.

Once we are clear that states, diplomats, and politicians no longer have a monopoly on the politics of war, we must recognize that exile groups, members of Congress, humanitarian voices, allied governments, religious groups all need to develop a politics about violence, for they all share in the nation's war powers. All will want to compare the use of force to other institutional alternatives. They will want to break the "military option" down into pieces, which can then be recombined with other modes of action. They will want "war" to be a matter of more or less—to ensure flexibility and to avoid overreacting should our adversaries cross one or another line in the sand. Law is often the instrument for unbundling, rearranging, and differentiating these various tactics—for arranging modes of political action that involve violence on a continuum with those that do not.

Law itself may also be an instrument of policy, on a continuum with war—different means to the same end. The military might be able to seize and secure territory, resources, or people. The application of military force might be able to break the will of a political adversary. The use of force might send a message—about our seriousness and resolve. Perhaps "they only understand force." Of course, it is not only the *use* of force that can do these things. Threats can work—even threats that someone else may resort to force, someone who will protect us, someone who will defy us but play into our hands, someone we control—or whom, unfortunately, we do not control. But law can sometimes do many of these things as well: seize and secure territory, resources, or people, send messages about resolve and political seriousness, even break the will of a political opponent. Doing these things violently or legally, or some other way altogether, will have different political significance, will engage different constituencies, encounter different obstacles. It is hard to imagine an effective international political initiative that does not rely on some mix of visible and latent violent and legal modes of authority. What may be most difficult to see is that to use law is also to invoke violence, at least the violence that stands behind legal authority. Asserting one's property rights, as every first-year law student learns, is to call, at least implicitly, on the enforcement arm of the state in one's relations with other private parties. The reverse is also true—to use violence is to invoke the law, the law that stands behind war, legitimating and permiting violence.

In another sense, as the international political system has become more disaggregated and chaotic, and as background elites have become more significant, the global political context for warfare has in other ways become far more unified and coherent than it was in the age of more independent and authoritarian nation-states. Debates about war—whether carried on in Sunday morning television talk shows, in diplomatic cables, corporate boardrooms, or local coffee shops—are increasingly conducted in a common global political language of appropriate and inappropriate national political and military objectives. The innumerable local and foreign constituencies that pull and tug at any national leadership nominally responsible for the use of military force are increasingly participating in a common conversation. The world's elites, whether in or out of government, are linked more closely together than ever before. They know one another. Political moods cross borders. Journalists, lawyers, or economists in different countries often speak the same language and share the same expertise. These links are a function of technology: the world's elites can and do meet one another and communicate with one another easily.

Increasingly, moreover, whether as cause or effect of all this connection, the world's elites share a common vocabulary for thinking about the legitimacy of political or military initiative. In many ways, this is not new. The German economist Wilhelm Röpke asserted in the 1950s that in the heyday of nineteenth-century liberalism the globe was ruled by what he termed the "As-If-World Government" constituted by the shared commitment of the world's ruling classes to the sharp separation of political and economic life.[2] The world, he claimed, had not needed a global organization or General Agreement on Tariffs and Trade to defend the liberal vision of open trade and finance against national governmental meddling precisely because all national elites already shared the sense that it was inappropriate to meddle with commerce. After Keynesian macroeconomic management became everywhere fashionable, he argued, institutions would be needed— for Europe, and for the world—to build down the habit of government intervention in the economic market. Whether Röpke had his nineteenth-century political and economic history right or not, there is no question that elite consensus about broad matters of economic policy has had an enormous transnational effect. For a while, all governments, right or left, were Keynesian, and then, after Thatcher and Reagan, the neoliberal "Washington Consensus" influenced what was and was not possible for varied political cultures across the globe. Perhaps the most significant recent example in the field of military affairs was the ability of the strategic studies profession to transform their computer models of prisoners in reiterated dilemmas into massive defense funding—in Moscow no less than Washington.

We have nevertheless tended to think that military affairs follow a different logic—a transhistorical logic of national interest, or a logic determined by military technology: the stirrup, the rifle, the machine gun, the tank. But a common vernacular among the world's elites about the appropriate ends and means of war can be as significant in shaping warfare as any consensus on the limits and appropriate means for economic policy. Is war the option of sovereign power—or does there need to be a reason? Must there be a particular kind of reason? Are there clearly inappropriate reasons—can one seize territory by conquest? Take foreign citizens as slaves? Military professionals have always had ideas about perfidy and treachery in warfare. Sometimes these ideas have been widely shared, and sometimes they have been subject to deep disagreement on different sides of a conflict.

The American military and those it has recently battled in Iraq, Afghanistan, and elsewhere have had different views about the tactics that seem perfidious. Attacking from mosques, dressing as civilians, recruiting suicide bombers—or bombing from thousands of feet, searching civilian homes, dividing the nation with cordons and checkpoints. The Israel Defense Forces and their Palestinian and other enemies also disagree deeply about the meaning of perfidy. What is striking, however, is the extent to which even enemies who stigmatize one another as not sharing in civilization nevertheless find themselves using a common vocabulary to dispute the appropriateness of military ends and means. This may arise in part from the dramatic ability of all participants in modern combat to speak about their means and ends to the same global audience.

The common vernacular for these inter- and intraelite conversations is increasingly provided by law. War today takes place on a terrain that is intensely governed—not by unified global institutions, but by a dense network of rules and shared assumptions among the world's elites. The domain outside and between nation-states is neither an anarchic political space beyond the reach of law, nor a domain of market freedom immune from regulation. Our international world is the product and preoccupation of an intense and ongoing project of regulation and management. Although it is easy to think of international affairs as a rolling sea of politics over which we have managed to throw but a thin net of legal rules, in truth the situation today is more the reverse. There is law at every turn—and only the most marginal opportunities for engaged political contestation. Seen sociologically, the official—and unofficial—footprint of national rules and national courts exceeds their nominal territorial jurisdiction. Tax systems, national public and private laws, financial institutions and payment systems, the world of private ordering—through contracts and corporate forms, standards bodies—all affect the behavior of public and private actors beyond their nominal jurisdictional reach. And that's just the beginning of international regulation. Of course, there is public international law, the United Nations, the world's trading regimes—it's a long list.

The power of experts and the density of law are linked. The world's professional elites are organized in legal institutions—corporations, foundations, universities. Their authority is rooted in their ability to interpret, manage, and enforce the hundreds of background norms and institutions that structure activity in the market, in the state, in the family. Their routine work establishes and refurbishes this complex transboundary legal and institutional milieu. At the same time, across the globe, experts communicate with one another in common vernaculars, their significance in every national system enhanced at the expense of conventional politicians by the processes we so often refer to as "globalization." The media through which they communicate have their own interest in adopting and promoting a common vocabulary among the elites who are the media's subject and its audience.

State power is everywhere spoken and exercised in the increasingly shared vocabulary of international relations, political science, international law, and military science. Wars and the machinery of war are ordered, purchased, launched, pursued in professional vocabularies, whether the computer-modeled rationality of nuclear deterrence, the justificatory language of humanitarian intervention, self-defense, and rights enforcement, or the gaming vernacular of dispute resolution and grand strategy. In this respect, state power is like international economic life, which is organized in the vocabulary of professions committed to growth and development, or like markets that are structured to reflect professional notions of "best practice" and defended in the professional language of efficiency. Indeed, the foreground sites we associate with political contestation and decision—the Oval Office, Congress—are also institutions whose debates are conducted, options framed, and programs designed in these common, often technical, vocabularies. To understand the politics of war and peace, we will need to understand the politics of the professions.

Professional War

When the president deploys the military, he is not simply pulling a lever. He is deploying an enormous and complex institutional machine, itself managed by a profession. War today is a function not only of the decisions of the statesmen whom we see taking political responsibility for the decision to go to war, but of innumerable experts and professionals working in the background of national and international political life. In his fascinating study of the post-1945 growth of the interlocking civilian and military complex of authority over the use of force, James Carroll puts it in this way: "At the Pentagon, bureaucracy replaced battle order as the defining social structure of the military."[3]

These professionals will have their own ideas about what war is, how it can and should be fought, when and how it can be ended. Perhaps they will have built their institutions, their professional doctrines and strategic rules of thumb to fight the "last war." Since 1945, for example, it has been argued that the American military remains organized to fight the type of large-scale campaign that characterized the Second World War, focused on seizing territory and defeating an enemy army rather than on the complex political, economic, and cultural maneuvers necessary to quell an insurgency or win the asymmetric wars of the postcolonial era. If so, this will limit what a president can accomplish with the military. In the same vein, it has been said that the U.S. military was unprepared for what came after the defeat of Saddam Hussein's army precisely because it had been reorganized for quick victory, followed by humanitarian assistance and diplomacy, rather than a drawn-out military effort to occupy the territory and crush resistance. We do not need to decide who is right to recognize the impact institutional habits and professional mind-sets can have on the course of war.

When the nation goes to war, moreover, it is not only the military profession that is mobilized. The humanitarians at home and abroad who make it their business to press for limits on the incidence and violence of warfare are also mobilized. And there are others—commercial and industrial professions, cultural and media professions, diplomatic professions, and more. I began studying the relationship between military and humanitarian professions to better understand, in simplest terms, the relationship between those focused on the politics of warfare from inside and those outside the institutional machinery of warfare—between those we would expect to defend the most expansive, and those who would advocate the most restrictive, approach to the use of force in particular circumstances. The more I have learned about their professional histories and specialized vernaculars, the more surprised I have been by the parallels between them, and the ways in which modern warfare has become the product of a complex dance between their different perspectives on a common set of issues. Increasingly, the rest of us are spectators, consumers, and bit players for a drama played out between these two mobilized professions.

Both are large and diverse professions. The military has soldiers and officers, logistics experts, military planners and strategists, and, of course, lawyers. They have various and complex relationships to their professional colleagues outside the military—in the jobs they left behind when called up, in the broader legal profession, in the rest of the government, among the civilian employees of the military, in defense contractors, and so forth. They are not, of course, cut off from civilian life. They watch the same media and are now linked to their families and colleagues at home by phone and Internet at even the most remote deployments. The humanitarian voices resisting a turn to war are also quite diverse, often including religious figures, media commentators, and pacifists of many sorts. The humanitarian profession includes the many human rights activists, media experts, and international lawyers who work for organizations like the International Committee of the Red Cross, Amnesty International, or Doctors Without Borders. Politicians or media elites who do not favor the war or who support the official party of opposition may also express themselves in humanitarian terms.

Of the two groups, the military is perhaps the more difficult to grasp for civilian students and academics, like myself, who have never served in uniform. For us, the military profession can seem a different universe. When I was young, the military and humanitarian professions could not have seemed more different. I registered as a conscientious objector after the Christmas bombings of Hanoi, and eventually became an international lawyer—I hoped I would find work promoting peace, economic development, and humanitarian and progressive values on the global stage. Nothing seemed as different as the humanitarian and military professions—the one made war, the other sought to limit war's incidence and moderate war's violence. Indeed, the military seemed to me then all that international law was not— violence and aggression to our reason and restraint.

As an international lawyer, I trained to be a professional outsider to warfare, an expert in human rights and humanitarian law, and in the rules that governed the global economy. When I studied history and political science, war and peace seemed utterly distinct: "Make peace, not war," was the slogan. For diplomatic historians, wars were fascinating, peace the space between them. For economic historians, the reverse was true. War, we learned, "broke out" when "disputes" could not be resolved peacefully, when cosmopolitan reason gave way to nationalist passion, when the normal "balance of power" was upset by abnormal statesmen. These bad-guy statesmen pursued outmoded projects of aggrandizement, domination, aggression, or imperialism. They were in cahoots with what we called "the military industrial complex"—not knowing we were quoting Eisenhower. The transnational commercial order promised to knit the world together in peace. We learned that no two nations in which one could buy a McDonald's hamburger had ever gone to war. What commerce could not achieve, the soft power and ethical clarity of international human rights and humanitarian law could.

"Realpolitik" was the disease; the softer wisdom of international law and international relations was the cure. The key to peace was *wise statecraft* and *conflict management*. We put our faith in negotiations among the disputing parties, which we hoped to facilitate. We were sure that reasonable aspirations for peaceful change should—and would—be accommodated by wise leaders, leaders who would act for the common good, in a global humanitarian and cosmopolitan spirit, and for whom we would serve as advisors. Leaders like that would address the roots of war in poverty, cultural backwardness, nationalist isolation, or ideological fervor. They would need—and want—help from the institutional machinery of the international community.

More than anything else, management for peace would require procedures—good practices, good offices, a steady and imaginative institutional framework, and a cadre of dedicated humanitarian policy experts who could express and implement the world's general interest in peace. All these would be designed, built, mandated, and managed by law. The

United Nations, the nongovernmental organizations, civil society—these peacemakers and peacekeepers needed to succeed so that the military would never again be needed. The world of rules, of procedures, of wise management would, should, sneak up on war, infiltrate the military, overwhelm the evil statesman, and make war a matter of the past. We would regulate swords into ploughshares.

Our image of the military came more from the movies than from experience. We laughed at their ceremony and hierarchy, felt uneasy about their training to kill. We thought of the military as something hot, passionate, engaged, while we were cooler heads, dry, focused—we were pragmatic and managerial. I think we imagined war as it is depicted in films of the ancient world. The troops mass at the border, a command is given, and everyone rushes forward helter-skelter, applying lethal force as fast and furiously as possible.

As aspiring humanitarians, law was not just a useful tool— we *desired* international law and the legal regulation of military conflict. If the military seemed irrational, the domain of unstrained violent desire, we sought in law a stern and rational hand, a fatherly limit. Where the military seemed the instrument of all too callous realists, we sought in law the expression of universal ethical verities. Where statesmen and the military leadership seemed prone to stumbling into conflict, we sought in law the institutions and procedures to slow things down and facilitate the communication we hoped would lead to wiser, more peaceful solutions to whatever differences brought the conflict to a head.

But, of course, war was not at all as we imagined it. The military was neither unreason nor self-interest unbound. Nor were military officers befuddled problem-solvers stumbling into conflict. Like us, they were professionals. They had blind spots, biases, professional deformations of the usual sort. But they were not passion to our reason, any more than they embodied national jingoism to our cosmopolitanism. War, no less than peace, must also be managed, by experts—even by cosmopolitan professionals. The more I have known military officers and military lawyers, the more obvious the parallels between our professions have become, and the more I've come to see us all as managers—with parallel passions. I've seen that when we differ, it is often the military who are the cooler heads.

Military professionals also have desires for law. For starters, they also turn to law to limit the violence of warfare, to ensure some safety, some decency, among professionals on different sides of the conflict. But making war has also become an extremely technical practice, involving the details of economic and social life, patterns of traffic and sewage and investment. For those of us outside the military who think about law *restraining* warfare, it is easy to overlook the many war-generative functions of law: the background rules and institutions for buying and selling weaponry, recruiting soldiers, managing armed forces, encouraging technological innovation, making the spoils of war profitable, channeling funds to and from belligerents or organizing public support. The military also turns to law to discipline the troops, to justify, excuse, and privilege battlefield violence, to build the institutional and logistical framework from which to launch the spear. The military profession seeks in law a vocabulary to frame the political environment in which war is to be fought and to regulate the division of labor between the military and civilian political or commercial elites in war. They also seek in law assurance that their killing is authorized and legitimate.

Some years ago, before the second war in Iraq, I spent some days on board the USS *Independence* in the Persian Gulf.

Nothing was as striking about the military culture I encountered there as its intensely *regulated* feel. Five thousand sailors, thousands of miles from base, managing complex technologies and weaponry, with constant turnover and flux. It was absolutely clear that even if you could afford to buy an aircraft carrier, you couldn't operate it. The carrier, like the military, is a social system, requiring a complex and entrenched culture of standard practices and shared experiences, of rules and discipline. The carrier is also a small town. I remember the eager salesman in a crowded mess hall selling Chevys for delivery when the crew next hit shore. I came away ready to believe that, at least in principle, no ship moves, no weapon is fired, no target selected without some review for compliance with regulation—not because the military has gone soft, but because there is simply no other way to make modern warfare work. Warfare has become rule and regulation.

Of course, neither humanitarians nor military planners desire law alone; they also hope there will be exceptions to law. When law permits violence, humanitarian voices often invoke a higher ethical vision, just as military leaders and statesmen often invoke national security to set aside legal limits on permissible force. Nor do they see in law only rules and clear procedures. Law is also a vocabulary of cunning and mendacity, promising to defend the indefensible and denounce the well accepted and legitimate. But the institutional pathways by which war is made—and resisted—have been carved in law.

Law as the Landscape for War

War is a legal institution because the institutions that fight— and those that seek to restrain the fight—are complex bureaucracies, managed by professionals. But the military and humanitarian professional also conduct their divergent campaigns in the shadow of endless background rules and institutions of public and private law, both national and international. We might call this "battling in the shadow of the law."

The parallels with other complex transnational activities is striking. Indeed, the more I have learned about the management of modern warfare, the more I have been reminded of the institutional challenges and routine practices of the transnational businessmen I encountered working as an international commercial lawyer. Managing a transnational supply chain is, in the end, not all that different from managing the logistics for war. When a business client contemplating a transnational commercial deal asks his or her lawyer, "What law will govern this deal?" the answer is anything but straightforward. Businessmen bargain in the shadow of all manner of law regulating contract and property, starting with private law. But which private law? Complex rules allocate competence for this or that aspect of the transaction to different national laws, state laws, local laws.

Then there is the national regulatory environment wherever the business will operate, and the national rules of whatever jurisdictions might seek to have—or simply turn out to have—transnational effects on the business. Much regulation is built into the transaction through private ordering. Perhaps industry standards or rules set by various expert bodies will have been internalized by a corporation, or forced down the supply chain through contract. And there might be some treaty law in there as well—the WTO, treaties of friendship and commerce, or other special bilateral arrangements.

When corporate lawyers assess the significance of all these laws for a business client, they look not only at the formal jurisdictional validity of various rules. They also assess their likely sociological effect—their likely impact on the client's business strategy. Who will *want* to regulate the transaction? Who will *be able to do so?* What rules will influence the transaction even absent enforcement? And they assess opportunities for the corporation to influence the rules, or to use them in new ways to achieve their strategic objective.

Military and humanitarian lawyers thinking about a particular campaign must also assess a changing legal environment. When an Italian prosecutor decides to charge CIA operatives for their alleged participation in a black operation of kidnapping and rendition, the law of the battlefield has shifted. The practice of military and humanitarian law requires complex and shifting predictions of fact and law. Whose *interpretation* of the law will, in fact, prevail, and before what audience?

Consequently, determining the law governing military operations is not a simple matter of looking things up in a book, particularly for coalition operations, or for campaigns that stretch the battlespace across numerous jurisdictions. The power of coalition partners—like the authority of our own military—will be limited by their legal authority. Their territorial authority will be a function of their legal claims. There will be private law, national regulation, treaties of various kinds, and more. For humanitarians, the national rules limiting military tactics will differ, as will the willingness of various jurisdictions to enforce legal rules. Figuring out where an alleged war criminal might be prosecuted is only the beginning, for several national jurisdictions have granted their courts jurisdiction to hear, and their prosecutors authority to bring, allegations against foreigners for acts committed abroad that allegedly violate shared rules of international law. But that does not mean it will be easy to get Pinochet or Kissinger or Sharon or Bin Laden or anyone else before a tribunal. Much will depend on the local and international political context. To say there is a rule or a court is only the beginning.

Baron de Jomini famously defined strategy as "the art of making war upon the map." Maps are not only representations of physical terrain, they are also legal constructs. Maps of powers, jurisdictions, liabilities, rights, and duties. When they have mapped the legal terrain, savvy businessmen do not treat the "law that governs" as static—they influence it. They forum shop. They bring test cases. They choose when to settle and when to litigate to maximize long-term gains, perhaps playing for favorable changes in the rules rather than results in particular cases. They structure their transactions to place income here, risks there. They internalize national regulations to shield themselves from liability. They lobby, they bargain for exceptions, they use the legal terrain strategically, structuring their deal not only in the shadow of the law, but to influence the law, to use the law as a commercial asset. We should not be surprised that human rights activists and professional humanitarians have learned to do the same. They forum shop, seek to influence the future development of rules, plead the most favorable interpretations of vague or uncertain rules.

Military planners also routinely use legal maps proactively to shape operations. When fighter jets scoot along a coastline, build to a package over friendly territory before crossing into hostile airspace, they are using the law strategically—as a shield, a marker of safe and unsafe. When they buy up commercial satellite capacity and commercially available satellite images of the battlefield so as to deny it to an adversary, contract is their weapon. They could presumably have denied their adversary access to those pictures in many ways. When the United States uses the Security Council to certify lists of terrorists to force seizure of their assets abroad, we might say that they have weaponized the law. Those assets might also have been immobilized in other ways. Military action has become legal action—just as legal acts have become weapons. Law is a strategic partner for the military when it structures logistics, command, and control, and smoothes the interface with all the institutions, public and private, that must be coordinated for military operations to succeed. It is a strategic partner for those who would restrict the military's options when it does not.

As humanitarian and military professionals work with the law of armed conflict, they change it. Of course the law that preexists a conflict constrains its course, conditioning expectations, establishing habits of mind and standard procedures of operation. Humanitarians and military professionals are used to thinking about influencing the law in peacetime, through careful negotiations, through codification, through advocacy, and through assertions of right. It can be hard, in combat, to see that the law is, if anything, more open to change. When humanitarian voices seize on vivid images of civilian casualties to raise expectations about the required accuracy of military targeting, they are changing the legal fabric.

In the Kosovo campaign, news reports of collateral damage often noted that coalition pilots could have improved their technical accuracy by flying lower—although this would have exposed their planes and pilots to more risk. The law of armed conflict does not require you to fly low or take more risk to avoid collateral damage; it requires you to avoid superfluous injury and unnecessary suffering. But these news reports changed the legal context—it seemed "unfair." Humanitarians seized the moment, developing various theories to demand "feasible compliance" and holding the military to technically

achievable levels of care. In conference after conference, negotiation after negotiation, representatives of the U.S. military
have argued that this is simply not "the law." Perhaps not, but
the effect of the legal claim is hard to deny.

Of course, the military also seeks to affect the legal context
through its public affairs activity and through its action on the
battlefield. Asserting a right to attack a given objective may induce defenders to tie up assets in its defense, regardless of
whether it is going to be attacked or not. Attacking—or not
attacking—a mosque is as much a message as a tactic on the
ground.

That legal rules and institutions provide the background
for military action is not new. But we should note the *fluidity*
and *diversity* of the legal context. Often more than one law
might apply, or one law might be thought to apply in quite
different ways. Indeed, strange as it may seem, there is simply
more than one law of armed conflict, as enforced by different
jurisdictions and as viewed by different participants. As a result, understanding the legal context for military action,
whether you are a military officer or a humanitarian activist,
requires a sophisticated exercise in *comparative* law. Different
nations—even in the same coalition—will have signed onto
different treaties. Different nations implement and interpret
common rules and principles differently.

The rules look different to a military professional anticipating battle against a technologically superior foe or to a person
living in a Palestinian refugee camp in Gaza than they do to an
American pilot. Everywhere, critics outside the military looking at the same rules may lean toward restrictive interpretations, while the military might lean towards greater freedom
of maneuver. In particular cases, these strategic considerations look different to those promoting and resisting a military

campaign, as they will look different to the U.S. military and to the enemies it fights. Although any of us might well dis-agree with one or another interpretation, we must recognize that the legal materials are elastic enough to enable diverse interpretations. Harnessing law as a strategic asset to strengthen or restrain the military requires the creative use of *legal pluralism*—and a careful assessment of the power those with different interpretations may have to influence the context for operations. The astonishing thing is that these are differences in *perspective* on a quite similar set of legal doctrines and politi-cal considerations.

Law and the Legitimacy of Military Operations

The common legal vocabulary used by so many different voices to articulate support for or opposition to a given mili-tary campaign has itself become a political vocabulary for as-sessing the legitimacy of military operations—and the political viability of the policy and interests for which war is the contin-uation. The best-known legal tools for defending and de-nouncing military action are provided by what have come to be known as the "law of force," itself an amalgam of "laws of war" distinguishing uses of force that are permissible (self-defense) and impermissible (crimes of aggression); and the "laws in war" or the "law of armed conflict" regulating conduct on the battlefield itself. Today, the United Nations Charter and the various international treaties regulating weapons and mili-tary conduct—including the so-called Geneva Conventions—are the most well known of such tools.

The significance and meaning of these legal instruments is, of course, a matter of some debate. Opponents of the Bush administration have routinely claimed that the United States has disregarded these rules, or has claimed that they are not applicable to the war on terror. This is not, strictly speaking, accurate. The Bush administration *has* argued for more restrictive interpretations of many of these international rules than had past administrations or than do many governments with which the United States is formally allied. But their arguments—the now famous internal memoranda of the justice department's Office of Legal Counsel—were professional arguments about how recognized rules and standards, as well as recognized exceptions and jurisdictional limitations, should be interpreted. They may have been politically ill-advised. They may have been professionally well argued or not. But they were professional arguments from a shared set of texts and historical precedents. To my mind, in fact, they took those texts all too literally, imagining that what could be done with words on the page would translate into viable legal—and political, and military—strategy. As professionals, these lawyers failed to advise their client adequately about the consequences of the interpretations they proposed, and about the way others would read the same texts—and their memoranda.

At a broader level, it has become routine to say that international law had little effect on the Iraq war: arguments by a few international lawyers that the war was illegal failed to stop the Bush administration and its allies, who were determined to go ahead regardless, and who had, after all, their own international lawyers to rely upon. But this lets international law off the hook too easily. The Bush and Blair administrations argued for the war in terms drawn straight from the UN Charter, and they issued elaborate legal opinions legitimating the invasion in precisely those terms. Opponents of the war were playing with the same deck. For both, it was the laws of war that provided the vocabulary for assessing the legitimacy of the campaign, for defending as well as attacking the "legality" of the war. If we expand the aperture from the decision to invade, the war looks even more to be a product of law. It was the traditional laws *in* war that were used to distinguish legitimate from illegitimate targets and to justify—or denounce—the inevitable "collateral" damage to Iraqi civilians.

We might think of law in this sense as part of what Clausewitz called "friction" in war—the innumerable factors that speed or impede operations. But if law can increase friction by persuading relevant audiences of a campaign's illegitimacy, it can also grease the wheels of combat. Law is a strategic partner for military commanders when it increases the perception of outsiders that what the military is doing is legitimate. And of course, it is a strategic partner for the war's opponents when it increases the perception that what the military is doing is not legitimate.

The result is an increasingly complex dance between the military professions and their humanitarian critics. For humanitarians, the routinization of humanitarian law into the military profession might well seem a profound achievement. The lawyers of the Red Cross might well be proud that the rules of engagement disciplining the application of force have taken on board so much from what began as external humanitarian standards. Military professionalism affirms civilian control. But humanitarian lawyers might also miss the experience of standing outside, speaking humanist truth to military power. We see something of this in the tension between lawyers for the Red Cross, making confidential visits to prisons and discussing their findings only with their military counterparts, and human rights activists bringing far more general norms to bear in more public settings. For the military planner, placing law in the war room might well improve discipline and smooth the political context for warfare—but what happens to the real-political necessity for the military to break some eggs when the going gets tough? Much as both professions have desired law, and worked to build a common legal vocabulary, they have not surrendered the option to insist upon an exception. Here, a higher ethics trumps what law would permit, sustaining public denunciation of military behavior for which there may well be a watertight legal defense. Or here, national security and the requirements of the campaign authorize the "black operation" of secret operatives and special forces.

The emergence of a common vocabulary—of rules and exceptions, broad standards and disputed interpretation—for military and humanitarian professionals assessing the legitimacy of warfare is a great accomplishment. That it should have become as well a common transnational vocabulary of political legitimacy—for understanding, pursuing, and defending political interests on the global stage—is certainly remarkable. That this vocabulary is itself a fluid and pluralistic one is troubling—but may also be the subtle secret of its success. This may well not have surprised Clausewitz, who continued his famous paragraph on war as a continuation of policy with a striking turn to language:

> The main lines along which military events progress, and to which they are restricted, are political lines that continue throughout the war into the subsequent peace. How could it be otherwise? Do political relations between peoples and between their governments stop when diplomatic notes are no longer exchanged? Is war not just another expression of their thoughts, another form of speech or writing? Its grammar, indeed, may be its own, but not its logic.[4]

Stepping back for a moment, we might worry about the fate of a more independent humanism—or about the erosion of a more autonomous military culture and tradition. We might worry about the legal "principle of distinction" itself— the principle that military and civilian professions *must* be distinguished. But before looking to the virtues and vices of the modern legal institution that warfare has become, however, we must understand something more of how we got here—and something of the reactions of the participants themselves.

It is not surprising that humanitarians and military commanders alike would sometimes resist the shared legalization of their increasingly parallel professions. From the humanitarian side of the fence, there is a loss in abandoning the image and sensibility of righteous outsiders, foreign to all things violent. It is easy, facing a violent political and military establishment, to wish for firm rules and clear distinctions—not for a loose common vocabulary of arguments and counter arguments. From the other side, it is normal that military commanders would be suspicious about embracing law as a strategic partner. When I was in corporate practice, I often saw the same suspicion among businessmen. Law, they said, was too rigid, looked back rather than forward. In their eyes, law was basically a bunch of rules and prohibitions—you figure out what you want to achieve, and then, if you have time, you can ask the lawyers to vet it to be sure no one gets in trouble.

You find the same thoughts in classics of military strategy. Here is Helmuth von Moltke:

> In war, as in art, there is no general norm; in both cases talent cannot be replaced by rules. General dogmas or rules

deduced from them or systems built upon them can therefore in no way have any practical value for strategy. Strategy is not like abstract sciences. Those have their fixed, defined truths on which one can construct arguments, from which one can make deductions.[5]

Von Moltke is talking about more than *legal* rules—he is attacking strategic doctrine that reduced the commander's judgment to mechanical rules and formal systems. Strategic vision, he insisted, must be *antiformal*—it requires creativity, innovation, flexibility.

Clausewitz's own skepticism about law was rooted in his commitment to the *political* character of warfare. Legal and social restraints on war stood outside politics. They were, he thought, rooted in ethics, in chivalry, in *politesse* and in notions about the distance between "civilization" and warfare. But if they could not bend political will to their ends, they could also not limit war. Already in the opening pages of *On War* he denigrates the idea that force might be limited by civilization—might itself be civilized.

If, then, civilized nations do not put their prisoners to death or devastate cities and countries, it is because intelligence plays a larger part in their methods of warfare and has taught them more effective ways of using force than the crude expression of instinct. [6]

In their time and place, Clausewitz and von Moltke were right. Eighteenth-century international law *was* rooted in ethics and in visions of natural justice. Nineteenth-century international law *was* formal and rule-oriented. It *was* abstract; legal scholars did try to elaborate a "scientific" doctrinal system, linking all the rules to a few general principles. In those days, law was proud of its separation from political, economic—and military—reality.

But this is no longer the case. For a century, law—and particularly international law—has been in revolt against formalism, and has sought in every possible way to become a practical vocabulary for politics. The revolt has been successful. Law has become more than the sum of the rules; it has become a vocabulary for judgment, for action, for communication. Most importantly, law has become a mark of legitimacy—and legitimacy has become the currency of power. Nevertheless, the potential to distinguish has not been eliminated; it is not all vague standards and interpretive differences. Instead, the relationship between war and peace has become, for the humanitarian lawyer and military professional, *itself* something to be managed. We now have the rhetorical—and doctrinal—tools to make and unmake the distinction between war and peace. And we do so as a tactic in both war and peace. The result is less a difference between the outside of humanitarian virtue and the inside of military violence than a common profession whose practitioners manage the relationship between war and peace within a common language—all the while working in the shadow of a new outside—the world we think of as "politics."

2 ✦ The Historical Context: How Did We Get Here?

We know that international politics, statecraft, and warfare have all been transformed since the Second Continental Congress sent Benjamin Franklin to France in 1776 to secure what assistance he could for the thirteen colonies in their war with Britain. Over the same years, law has also been dramatically rethought and remade. Statecraft, warfare, and law each has its own history, to be sure, but their stories also overlap and have influenced one another. To understand law's contemporary function as a vernacular of political judgment, we need to pay particular attention to changes in ideas about law that came after von Moltke and Clausewitz dismissed its relevance to war. So long as politics and law were distinct, Clausewitz was right—war as politics trumps law. As law has bled into politics in the years since, however, war has become, in Clausewitzian terms, the continuation of law by other means.

In legal history, the narrative line in this very complex story is actually quite simple—the rise and fall of a traditional legal world that sharply distinguished war from peace and in which law was itself cleanly distinguished from both morality and politics. This traditional world lasted only a half century. It rose in the mid–nineteenth-century as earlier faith in a universal order of morality or right reason gave way to faith in legal science and the "positivism" of legal deference to sovereign authority. This traditional legal system was already declining in the years after the First World War, although it continued to influence thinking about war until deep into the twentieth-century and still provides the rhetorical material for making a variety of distinctions, including those between declared war and other uses of force, between combatant and civilian, belligerent and neutral, combat and occupation, or the public and private use of force.

Our modern legal vernacular shows traces of all three periods. There are ethical invocations and considerations of policy reminiscent of the preclassical period, sharp doctrinal boundaries and images of absolute sovereign power reminiscent of the classical period, as well as more continuous institutions and fluid standards of behavior that blur the boundaries between war and peace, or legal and political action. The result is often a confusing mix of distinctions that can melt into air when we press on them too firmly: a law of firm rules and loose exceptions, of foundational principles and counterprinciples, pitched as a vocabulary of ethics and savvy political calculation.

International Law before the Rise of Modern War and Statecraft

There were, of course, legal ideas about war long before the traditional international legal system of the late nineteenth-century. When commentators wish to stress law's role—actual or potential—as the reservoir of enduring ethical principles and visions of "justice," they begin the story far earlier. A number of scholars from the sixteenth and seventeenth centuries have come to be seen as canonical precursors for— or founders of—modern international law, among them the Catholics Francisco de Vitoria (1480–1546) and Francisco Suárez (1584–1617), and the Protestants Alberico Gentili (1552–1608) and Hugo Grotius (1583–1645).[1] In their work, you will find a variety of ideas about "just war," as well as quite specific legal rules about the procedures a prince must go through (including consulting with experts) to determine the justice of his cause, and the conduct permitted in and after battle. These early legal texts drew heavily on religious thinking—indeed, they were sometimes written by religious scholars and officials. They certainly grappled with issues that continue to be posed by the discipline of international law, but they do so in a fashion so dissimilar from later work that historians who focus on these texts as "founders" of modern international law distort their distinctive voice.

Unlike the traditionalists who followed, these early writers did not distinguish between legal and moral authority, or between national and international law, or between the public and private capacities of sovereign authorities. In all these ways, sixteenth-century legal ideas about war would come to seem naive by the late eighteenth and early nineteenth centuries. For the international lawyer today, by contrast, the traditional texts of the late nineteenth-century seem to assert all these distinctions too emphatically—even as the earlier scholars seemed oddly unaware of their importance.

Whereas traditional international law scholars sharply distinguished moral and legal authority, for the earlier scholars, they bled easily into one another. Natural law, international law, civil law, divine law—all were part of the same soup. In that world, the nineteenth-century idea that a sovereign could be bound by a particular rule as a matter of conscience, but not as a matter of law, made no sense. Nor do the early scholars distinguish domestic law from international law, or the law that binds sovereigns in their relations with one another from that which binds their citizens or themselves in their relations with their citizens. Rather, the early texts envision a single law that covers sovereigns and citizens alike. It was only later that the national rules governing sailors on a naval vessel would come to seem part of a different legal order from international legal discussions about sovereign authority to make war. In the earlier period, ideas about self-defense from civil law, religious thoughts about humility and mercy, and ideas from Roman law about citizenship could all be found transposed into discussions of intersovereign relations. Although sovereigns and citizens may be bound by different rules (the sovereign may have a higher duty to inquire into the justice of war, for example, than the citizen), these differences seemed to flow from differing capacities within a unified moral-legal system.

Before we get too nostalgic for the faith of our ancestors, however, we should remember that their law was not only an ethical limit on military power. It was also a license. The sixteenth-century Spanish jurist Francisco de Vitoria, for example, famously took it for granted that the Indians whom the conquistadors discovered in what was becoming the Spanish empire were covered by the same moral/legal order as the Spanish. As a result, however, the Indians found themselves subject to obligations, and to penalties for their violation. For example, although Indian title to the lands they occupied was legitimate public title, the Indian title holders were subject to the universal moral order requiring sovereigns to permit free intercourse and propagation of the faith. When the Spanish arrived to put the gospel clearly to them, any attempt by the Indians to violate these divinely revealed "rights" terminated their title and enabled the Spaniards to use whatever force seemed necessary to enforce the divine order. According to Vitoria,

> If, after the Spaniards have used all diligence, both in deed and in word, to show that nothing will come from them to interfere with the peace and wellbeing of the aborigines, the latter nevertheless persist in their hostility and do their best to destroy the Spaniards, they can make war on the Indians, no longer as an innocent folk, but as against forsworn enemies, and may enforce against them all the rights of war, despoiling them of their goods, reducing them to captivity, deposing their former lords and setting up new ones, yet withal with observance of the proportion as regards the nature of the circumstance and of the wrongs done to them. This conclusion is sufficiently apparent from the fact that, if it be lawful to declare the war, it is consequently lawful to pursue the rights of war.[2]

For other sixteenth-century scholars, the rights of the just warrior were even more vigorously absolute, in combat and after victory.

By the late eighteenth and early nineteenth centuries, the law of nations had begun to emerge as a more distinct branch of legal thought. One of its champions was the Swiss scholar Emerich de Vattel, whose 1758 treatise *The Law of Nations: or Principles of the Law of Nature Applied to the Conduct and Affairs of Nations and Sovereigns: a Work Tending to Display the True Interest of Powers* became the most influential work for

American statesmen and jurists through the mid–nineteenth-century. The work was translated and reprinted in numerous editions, and famously recommended by Benjamin Franklin to his contemporaries as the appropriate internationally oriented companion volume to William Blackstone's *Commentaries on the Laws of England* (1765–69) for guidance in governing the new nation.

Vattel begins by asserting the field's distinctive character, marking a respectful distance from Grotius in the following terms:

> If therefore from the idea that political societies or nations live, with respect to each other, in a reciprocal independence in the state of nature and that they are subject as political bodies, to the Law of Nature, had Grotius moreover considered, that the law ought to be applied to these new subjects, in a manner suitable to their nature, this judicious author would have acknowledged, without difficulty, that the natural Law of Nations is a particular science: that by this law is produced even an *external* obligation between nations, independently of their volition; and that the consent of different states is only the foundation and source of a kind of particular law, called the *Arbitrary Law of Nations*.[3]

Vattel's confidence that a universal natural law bound all nations, "independently of their volition," was shared by statesmen and jurists until late in the nineteenth-century. One need only read Justice Marshall's Supreme Court opinions about everything from slavery to Indian land claims to realize how obvious it seemed to the American elite that statecraft took place within a preexisting legal culture—precisely as the common law continued to bind citizens of the new nation.

But it is hard to make sense of Vattel's table of contents today, or to understand its appeal as a sensible, rigorously reasoned, guide for statesmen who wished to participate in the existing international order. Too many things we now regard as distinct are mixed together, giving modern readers the impression that Vattel just did not reason in a very clear or rigorous way. His book mixes together topics we would treat as part of national constitutional law, international law, political ethics, religious doctrine, private law, and more. Ideas about good government, the purpose and ethics of rulership and the philosophy of public authority are interspersed with propositions about the rights of "regents" and the "utility of tillage" for the cultivation of the earth or the "nature of the right of buying," and the desirability of monopolies. Observations bearing on statecraft in war appear throughout the volume—among the objects and obligations of "good government," as a component in the "advantages of glory" for the nation, and among the "common Duties of a Nation toward others, or of the offices of Humanity between Nations" and his enumeration of the rights and obligations related to the "observation of justice between nations." What we would think of as the "use of military force" pops up as a legal remedy for wrongs suffered in the law of retortion and reprisal, as well as in the law explicitly relating to what Vattel terms "war." War, moreover, for Vattel, may itself be public or private.

If we read this fluid movement between considerations of morality, policy, and right as sloppy thinking, it will be easy to dismiss Vattel's advice to statesmen. But in another way, there is something oddly contemporary about his approach—as if the world *before* the emergence of all these distinctions shared something with our own world after these distinctions have unraveled. Vattel remarks in a quite general way on the "terrible effects" of war, "its destructive and unhappy consequences," and observes that the choice of war "should never be undertaken without the strongest reasons," before he considers the "just causes of war."[4] The "justificatory reasons" he develops mix considerations of legal right with what we would think of as wise statecraft and ethical virtue in rulership. At one point he notes that "the right of using force or making war, belongs to nations no farther than is necessary to their defence, and the support of their rights" (ibid., 369), and at another, "I call decent and commendable motives those derived from the good of the state, from the safety and common advantage of the citizens" (ibid., 370). He excoriates the sovereign who goes to war "without reason" as "responsible to God, and accountable to man, for every person that is killed" (ibid., 369).

> The violence, the crimes, the various disorders attendant on the licentious tumult of arms, pollute his conscience and blacken his account, and he is the original author of them all. May this faint sketch affect the heart of the leaders of nations and in military enterprises suggest to them a circumspection proportional to the importance of the subject! (Ibid., 369)

He advises statesmen as follows:

> [A]n unjust war may for a time enrich a nation, and enlarge its frontiers, but it thereby becomes odious to other nations, and is in danger of being oppressed by them. Besides, do opulence and extent of dominion always constitute the happiness of states? Amidst the multitude of instances which offer themselves here, I shall confine myself to the Romans. The Roman republic ruined itself by its triumphs, the excess of its conquests and power. Rome, the mistress of the world,

when enslaved by tyrants, and oppressed by a military government, had reason to deplore the success of its arms, and to look back with regret on those happy times when its power did not reach beyond Italy, or even when its dominion was almost confined within the circuit of its walls.

The unjust motives are all such as have no tendency to produce the good of the state, which, instead of being drawn from that pure source, are suggested by the violence of passions. Such are the arrogant desire of command, the ostentation of power, the thirst of riches, the avidity of conquest, hatred and revenge. (Ibid., 371)

In short, Vattel offers us a meditation on power and policy as well as right. There is no question war may be fought to defend the state, enforce its rights, and revenge wrongs against the nation. But Vattel offers a mixed rhetoric of law and virtue that can sound familiar to modern ears.

Nations which are always ready to take arms on any prospect of advantage, are lawless robbers: but they who seem to delight in the ravages of war, who spread it on all sides, without any other motives than their ferocity, are monsters unworthy of the name of men. They should be considered as the enemies of mankind, in the same manner as in civil society. Assassins and incendiaries by profession, are not only guilty in respect of the particular victims of their violences, but likewise of the state to which they are declared enemies. All nations have a right to join in punishing, suppressing, and even exterminating these savages. (Ibid., 372)

Perhaps most strikingly, Vattel's idea that his advice will find its confirmation in the consequences wrought by *other* states on the sovereign who neglects his advice also foreshadows current thinking about law as a vernacular of legitimacy. Earlier scholars had puzzled about the difficulties posed for a doctrinal scheme by the possibility that a war might be—or seem to be—just on both sides. It would certainly often be the case that two sovereigns would think their cause just. For Vattel, this poses no particular problem. The proof will be in the response of other powers.

> It may however happen, that both the contending parties act with candor, and in a doubtful cause it is still uncertain which side is in the right. Nations then being equal and independent . . . so as not to claim a right of judgment over each other; it follows that in every case susceptible of doubt, the arms of the two parties at war are to be accounted equally lawful at least as to external effects, and till the decision of the cause. This does not hinder other nations from judging it for themselves, for knowing what they have to do, and assisting that nation which shall appear to have right on its side. (Ibid., 374)

It is not surprising that for Vattel, the purpose of a declaration of war—as of the requirement that war *be* declared—is one of policy, rather than of marking the separation between distinct legal regimes of war and peace, or neutrality and belligerency.

> [I]t is possible that the present fear of our arms may make an impression on the mind of an adversary, and induce him to do us justice. . . . We owe this farther regard to humanity, and especially to the lives and tranquility of the subjects, to declare to this unjust nation, or its chief, that we at length are going to have recourse to the last remedy, and

make use of open force, for bringing him to reason. This is called *declaring war.* (Ibid., 383)

The various subdoctrines of the obligation to declare war flow from this purpose—the declaration must be made *to the state* against which war will follow, need not be made in defensive wars, nor must it be made in a way that would "allow the enemy time to prepare itself for an unjust defense" (ibid., 384).

One can imagine statesmen consulting Vattel about the wisdom and justice of their military campaigns. Franklin thought his advice to aspiring national leaders wise and useful. The advice of the jurist might blend easily with that of the Enlightenment clergyman or philosopher. Law offered a discourse of wise policy, precedent, accepted practice, and strategic counsel for statesmen participating in a well-understood and accepted transnational discussion of good governance.

Law Meets Modern Warfare

It is difficult, however, to imagine Napoleon getting much out of Vattel. Vattel wrote for those, like Franklin, who aspired to be wise statesmen for nations participating in an established international order—not those who wished to revolutionize that order. Revolutionary statesmen would march to a different drummer. Napoleon transformed warfare as much as statecraft. His levee en masse inaugurated a new mode of national war that would come to mobilize the full industrial and economic power of the nation behind the massive conscript armies of the First World War. In that century, moreover, legal conceptions of sovereigns were also transformed, eliminating the presumption that national elites exercised power subject to a well-understood regime of international norms.

To understand the emergence of the modern law about war requires that we revisit the process by which the traditional international legal thought of the nineteenth-century developed, alongside these changes in the nature of warfare and statecraft. The traditional laws of war—of the late nineteenth-century—were forged in the shadow of the new conception of warfare and statecraft whose inauguration we associate with Napoleon. In the late eighteenth and early nineteenth centuries, what had been an aristocratic endeavor of the old regime became the general project of a nation—an extension of public policy, an act of the whole.

This is the development crystallized by Clausewitz as a continuity between war and peace. We have come to treat his formulation as classic:

> We know, certainly, that War is only called forth through the political intercourse of Governments and Nations; but in general it is supposed that such intercourse is broken off by War, and that a totally different state of things ensues, subject to no laws but its own. We maintain, on the contrary, that War is nothing but a continuation of political intercourse, with a mixture of other means.[5]

The new attitude Clausewitz proposes had been building for a generation. But the revolutionary break with the ancien régime—and the Napoleonic wars that followed—drove it home. The transformation of war from the interpersonal, dynastic, and religious struggles of an aristocracy to the public struggles of a nation—a citizens' army, the army "of the republic"—made war visible as an extension of national policy, a project of the whole society.

As war became continuous with the political intercourse of peacetime, it also became the public affair of a nation, an instrument of national policy, an expression of national sovereignty, a sign of national honor. The ancient marks of military distinctiveness—the uniform, the profession, the codes of honor—took on a new significance, signaling not aristocratic status, but participation in national public life, and, increasingly, submission to civilian leadership.

Latent in the Clausewitzian merger of war and public policy lay a distinction between the old war and the new—wars of chivalry, honor, and passion, versus wars of reason, calculation, and policy. Vattel's sovereigns would use war to settle disputes, defend their possessions and tranquility, or right wrongs against a shared order. When Clausewitz uses the word "politics," he has in mind a far broader set of potential goals. After Napoleon, the political aims of war may well include the revolutionary overthrow of the order itself. Military thinking would need to adjust to the emergence of political leaders unbound.

Once the legitimate objectives of statecraft were unleashed from the shared objectives of the ancien régime, they might or might not be revolutionary—but they were now all political, a term that increasingly came to mean "whatever is determined by the leaders of a nation to be their objective." Henry Kissinger described nineteenth-century warfare as a series of political initiatives bracketed by the revolutionary moments of the Napoleonic wars and the First World War.

In the intervals between those explosions of maximum violence, war was considered an extension of policy. Between the Congress of Vienna in 1815 and the outbreak of World

War I, wars were limited by the political objectives of the opponents. Because they were fought for specific goals which did not threaten the survival of any of the powers, a reasonable relationship existed between the force employed and the objective to be achieved.[6]

At the same time, the legal terms for understanding the origins of war focused on the sovereign's power to make war, rather than the appropriate reasons that might move a well-educated statesman to make war. Vattel's varied considerations of ethics, obligation, right, and good governance had given way to a far more focused idea about political interests and national policy objectives: the will of the sovereign. War is no longer the outbreak of passion, defense or vindication—it has become an instrument of reason in pursuit of the nation's political goals.

It took some time for this new vision to take hold. In 1838, a few years after Clausewitz wrote, and long before he would became a wartime president, Abraham Lincoln spoke of the abolitionist cause in these terms:

> Passion has helped us, but can do so no more. It will in future be our enemy. Reason, cold calculating, unimpassioned reason, must furnish all the materials for our future support and defense.[7]

In saying this, Lincoln was understood to set himself against war—the just cause would need the calm determination of cooler peacetime heads. Two and a half decades later, however, Lincoln would be embroiled in a war that would confound this easy opposition of passionate war and reasoned peace.

Our Civil War—birthplace for so much of the law in war— is often remembered as the first "modern" war. In part, this is winner's history—a war of the modern North against the ante-bellum South, a war of industrial power and the federal na-tion, against the old military order of chivalry and the old sec-tarianism of region. A culture of commerce defeated a culture of honor, cold Northern reason slowly quenching the hot pas-sions of the South in the name of a National Whole.

But the Civil War's modernity lay not only in the Northern victory. For both sides, this was a war pitting the full economic and spiritual powers of their imagined community against an-other in a struggle for national identity. It was modern war as *total* war, war of the whole, war for the whole. For Kissinger, the American Civil War was an exception to the long century of politically limited war—it "approached the status of a total war precisely because it was a revolutionary struggle."[8]

In this sense, Lincoln's unimpassioned reason would not forestall war, it would become war. But neither would it re-main split from passion, as Lincoln's inspired vocabulary of sacrifice, sanctification—"we cannot dedicate, we cannot con-secrate, we cannot hallow this ground"—would attest.

More than anything, the modernity of the Civil War lay in the strange brew of reason and passion through which the struggle was understood by both sides. The Northern cause was also a crusade, the Southern military also a redoubt of professional skill, thought, art, against an often brutal Northern campaign. The rhetorical tools for distinguishing war and peace, new wars and old wars, were there—but they were redirected to define the relations between the warring parties. This mix of passion, reason, and national expression on both sides conjured up a war of singular ferocity. In a sense, the Clausewitzian vision had now been fully realized—war had become continuous, in reason *and* passion, with the great political struggles of the nation, and with national identity itself.

On the one hand, it might seem that by merging war with politics, the theory and practice of warfare had come into line with Vattel's quite fluid conception of the ethical, legal, and policy considerations that ought to guide statesmen in thinking about war. Meanwhile, however, in the field of law, Vattel's ideas were being replaced with a mode of legal thought that differentiated legal criteria from political and ethical considerations far more sharply. Just as Clausewitz was bringing politics and war together, jurists were forcing law and politics apart. The result would be a law standing outside the domain of politics and war—and a politics unleashed from legal and ethical constraint.

Nevertheless, nineteenth-century legal developments also contributed to the emerging vision of warfare. The private modes of warfare associated with the old regime were progressively eliminated. The 1856 Paris Declaration, for example, eliminated "privateering," a complex legal institution through which "letters of marque" authorized private vessels to carry out belligerent acts. They seemed incompatible with new legal conceptions of sovereignty that stressed its legal status as a unitary public authority exercising a monopoly of military force. Henceforth there would be one sovereign, one military.

Over the course of the nineteenth-century, legal scholars placed the authority of sovereigns at the center of a reimagined legal order replete with formal distinctions. The earlier authors—from Grotius to Vattel—rarely spoke of "sovereigns" at all. All sorts of entities had rights—rulers of many different kinds, individuals, citizens, pirates, merchants. Later would come the East India Tea Company. The key elements in the system were *rights* and *wrongs*, not sovereigns. All these players had rights and powers and obligations that often moved with them from place to place. When earlier jurists had focused on the sovereign, it had seemed obvious that only the just and right public acts of sovereigns were legitimate; a prince acting for personal greed acts unjustly and hence illegitimately, and wars for private empire are therefore also unjust, end of story.

By the late nineteenth-century, international jurists *begin* their analysis with the sovereign act. In such a world, it was easy to suggest that all wars publicly declared by a sovereign were just; the point was to discover if this was the sovereign, and if the war was the product of his public act. By contrast, earlier scholars began the analysis with an idea about justice, grounded in a moral/legal order that defined sovereignty and the capacities of sovereigns. Justice entrusts sovereigns with certain prerogatives, among them the capacity to engage in wars. Private wars do not express these just sovereign capacities and are therefore unjust. The nineteenth-century scholar begins with a conception of sovereign authority and seeks to elaborate its legal competence, while the earlier scholar began with a notion of moral and legal justice from which he elaborated the capacities of sovereigns.

In the nineteenth-century legal imagination, the sovereign marked the boundary between different legal universes— international and national, as well as public and private. The domestic and international legal orders were separated by the different faces of sovereign power at home and abroad. The domestic realm came to be imagined as a vertical legal order of sovereign powers and citizen rights. The international legal order was thought of as a horizontal order among sovereign authorities, allocating jurisdictions and building order among independent sovereigns by contract. The sovercign was the source of vertical authority at home, and had the (often exclusive) capacity for horizontal contract internationally. His two capacities form the boundary between the two legal spheres—he acts *either* internally or externally.

This scheme transposed the relationship between public and private law in the national legal system to the global level by analogy. Domestically, the private law world of contract and property was understood as a horizontal order of individuals with rights, building legal relationships by consent. In the public sphere, by contrast, law was a vertical affair of public powers enforced upon those subject to the sovereign's jurisdiction. Sovereigns—and citizens—had powers and exercised rights that came to seem absolute within their respective spheres: freedom of contract for individuals in the private sphere and police powers for the state in the public sphere. The function of the legal order, broadly conceived, was to keep these spheres distinct, and ensure that legal actors exercised the powers and rights appropriate to their sphere.

For the sovereign this meant something quite different domestically and internationally. Domestically the sovereign exercised public "police" powers, delegated by national constitutional arrangements. When acting publicly in the international realm, the sovereign was the unrestrained political origin for law itself, and could make war as an unrestrained exercise of sovereign power. Nevertheless, in both spheres, the sovereign must respect private right. As a result, the classical jurist paid a great deal of attention to the boundaries between the spheres. By policing the boundaries among the spheres, the legal order could ensure the possibility of tranquility of each. It was during this classical period that war became a distinct legal status, in which public actors were said to have altogether different rights and powers than during peacetime.

Changes in Legal Thought:
An Opening for Humanitarianism

These late-nineteenth-century changes in legal consciousness transformed what it meant for war to be the exclusive act of a public sovereign. Emerging legal ideas influenced the way in which Clausewitz's assertion of the continuity between politics and war would be understood—by changing how politics and public power were themselves understood. By the end of the nineteenth-century, to think of war as the continuation of politics by other means no longer meant that war was continuous with peace, or a project of the *whole* nation—more the opposite.

For one thing, the emergence of sharp distinctions in legal thought between public and private brought with it the image of a transnational commercial space that should be kept free from contamination by public force. Private armies, mercenaries, privateers—all these were outmoded, not only because they were part of an aristocratic past, but because they did not fit with the new, exclusively *public* nature of sovereign war. The public realm had become one sphere of power among many, marked off from the private realm of the market and the family. Public warfare that had seemed general, continuous with the whole society, now seemed, in legal terms, specific—the project of the *government*, not the society. Similarly, the emergence of a sharp distinction between international and domestic spheres of authority suggested that sovereigns acting internationally could not disturb the domestic order in the territory of other sovereigns—except during war. The result was a sharp distinction between war and peace, and between belligerent and neutral powers. At war, sovereigns possessed unrestrained authority; at peace, they displayed respect for the domestic jurisdiction of other sovereigns. In such a system, the declaration of war will play a completely different function—marking the line between legal regimes.

Humanitarian voices supported the legal separation of war from the domain of peace. Broad pacifist campaigns arose from diverse sources: from church leaders, proponents of woman's suffrage, heirs to the abolition movement; as well as from political activists of all types: from anarchists, socialists, populists, progressives, Catholics. These diverse voices marked the distinction between war and peace in various ways—as ethics against politics, as faith against the cruel logic of commerce, as calm reason against fanaticism, as modern logic against the primitive culture of honor. In fact, the terms with which they marked the line between peace and war parallel those by which both sides distinguished North and South.

All these voices spoke to war, to the statesmen and military who made war, from outside—in the name of an alternative ethical vision—sometimes national, more often universal. War and peace were separate; Clausewitz was now the problem. We might now say they pled for peace by speaking truth to power. The point was to shrink the domain of war through moral suasion, agitation, shaming, and proselytizing. In their view, blurring war with peace was both dangerous and immoral.

This conviction lent an ethical urgency to the emergence of a sharp *legal* distinction between war and peace. Each was now a legal status, separated by a declaration. Combatants and noncombatants, neutrals and belligerents have different bundles of legal rights and privileges. The battlefield, the territory of belligerency, was legally demarcated. The legal treatises of the period began to place the law of peace and the law of war in separate volumes. In part, these distinctions aimed to limit the carnage of war by expanding the privileges of civilians and limiting the military privilege to kill.

These humanitarian limitations on war were thus part of a broader reorganization of legal thought, sharpening the distinction between the public and the private sphere, hardening private rights and limiting public powers to their respective spheres. For all that peace and war were to be legally separated, *private rights*, for example, were increasingly thought to be continuous across the boundary. It is here that we began to see the logic of thinking that when the dust settles after a war claiming the lives of millions, destroying empires, and remaking the political and economic landscape of the planet, people might reasonably feel they are still entitled to get their property back.

In short, the late nineteenth-century developed an alliance between two rather different sets of ideas: a humanitarian moral conviction that the forces of peace stand outside war, demanding that swords be beaten into ploughshares, and a legal project to sharpen the distinction between public powers and private rights. The result was a legal conception of war as a public project *limited to its sphere.* The legal distinctiveness of war reinforced the idea that war was itself a discrete and limited phenomenon—over there, the domain of combat. It seemed reasonable to expect that warriors *stay* over there, and that protected persons, even women soldiers, stay *outside* the domain of combat.

This alliance of ethics and legal form—together discontinuous from public policy and war—has continued across the twentieth-century and is with us still. We see it in the effort to restrain war by emphasizing its moral *and legal* distinctiveness—

by walling it off from peace and shrinking its domain. We see its echo in the many varieties of twentieth-century pacifism, in modern efforts to revive "just war" theory as an exogenous truth that can limit military power, and in the struggle to bring the language of human rights to bear on the military—to judge the effects of war by a different, higher, ethical standard. But we also see it in efforts to treat combat and "police action" as fundamentally—ethically, legally—different, the one the domain of human rights, the other the proper domain of the law of armed conflict.

Nevertheless, to contemporary jurists, the nineteenth-century distinctions seem arcane and lacking in nuance, while the earlier faith in a universal moral/legal order seems naive. In the twentieth-century, as the sovereign lost his central place as the boundary among legal spheres, the legitimacy of his various acts was no longer a technical or procedural matter of doing the right thing in the right way in the right sphere. The notion that a public declaration by a sovereign marks the boundary between war and peace now seems unduly formal and remarkably out of touch with the play of forces within and without sovereign territories that generate interstate violence. At the same time, the earlier notion that the public and communal acts of sovereigns are automatically legitimate now seems both to overestimate the power of the legal order to confer legitimacy and to ignore the importance of functional differences between acting publicly and privately, in war or in peace. Modern international lawyers have abandoned the nineteenth-century scholar's focus on the sovereign without recovering the earlier faith in a unified social/moral order. They have replaced a law of distinctions with what seems a more pragmatic unbundling of governmental action on both sides of the war/peace and public/private divides.

International Institutions and the
Rise of a Modern Law of Force

Indeed, over the course of the twentieth-century, humanitarians wishing to restrain the incidence and violence of warfare lost confidence in the strategy of standing with law outside of military and political power, insisting on respect for formal boundaries. This erosion in confidence was sped by the decline of the legal consciousness with which this strategy had been allied. Nevertheless, the legal consciousness of the classical era continued to influence many in the American foreign policy establishment.[9] Every American secretary of state from 1889 to 1945 was a lawyer, and for many of them, the broad ethos of the classical era provided the backdrop to their diplomacy. Until quite late in the twentieth-century, the classic legal sensibility continued to influence those in the American foreign policy establishment—most Republicans and many centrist Democrats—who saw foreign affairs as a domain for commercial stability more than as an arena for transformative or revolutionary politics.

Coming to the international scene, lawyers influenced by the legal thought of the classical period were oriented to the increasingly dense world of transnational private and commercial affairs, rather than to the diplomatic management of war. War was something that could be avoided by a combination of American "neutrality" and care to avoid foreign political entanglements. Law promised a neutral technique for recognizing the legitimate boundaries of sovereign authority. Men like Manley Hudson and Elihu Root worked tirelessly for the professional codification of international rules and the use of legal arbitration to resolve international disputes on the theory that sovereign interests, properly defined and understood, would converge. They were not isolationists by any means, but the terms of their engagement with the world—and the world they saw to be engaged—would not have been recognizable to Franklin, still less to Clausewitz. For them, the distinctions of classical international law seemed as reliable a guide to public diplomacy as to international private order, so long as boundaries were respected and disputes resolved through arbitration.

In a world of strict legal boundaries among powers, it was easy to imagine that the—legitimate—interests of sovereigns did not conflict in any unbridgeable way. Although it did seem doubtful, after the First World War, that warfare could be controlled by elaborating the entailments of a *legal status* or by relying on the coincidence of interests among sovereigns absolute only within legally defined spheres, arbitration did continue to seem promising where disputes concerned legal matters. Many interwar lawyers thought that many, even most, international disputes could be seen as differences of opinion about what sovereigns were *entitled* to; once their entitlements were neutrally clarified, the dispute might be resolved. In a sense, these lawyer-diplomats had regained something of Franklin's faith in the stability of a legally organized international establishment. For these lawyer-statesmen, international politics and law remained distinct realms. The bulk of disputes among sovereigns could yield to patient legal assessment and arbitration—for the rest, the traditional tools of diplomacy, coupled with a foreign policy of detachment from European internecine conflicts, would serve.

The disinterest of these men in matters of war, and their sense that legal arrangements were the natural stuff of diplomacy, is suggested by the story Elihu Root, by far the most prominent American international lawyer of his generation, told about his appointment as secretary of war by President McKinley.

> I was called to the telephone and told by one speaking for President McKinley, "The President directs me to say to you that he wishes you to take the position of Secretary of War." I answered, "Thank the President for me, but say that it is quite absurd, I know nothing about war, I know nothing about the army." I was told to hold the wire, and in a moment there came back the reply, "President McKinley directs me to say that he is not looking for any one who knows anything about war or for any one who knows anything about the army; he has got to have a lawyer to direct the government of these Spanish islands, and you are the lawyer he wants."[10]

The problem was that their established legal order was, in fact, being transformed by war and revolution. The First World War and the Russian Revolution shocked the world's elites on a scale not experienced since Napoleon. In part, the shock was the escalation of warfare into a force that transcended any conception of political interest that may have motivated it. Raymond Aron put it this way:

> Perhaps major wars are precisely those which, by reason of the passions they release, ultimately escape the men who have the illusion of controlling them. Retrospectively, the observer does not always perceive the conflict of interests that would have justified the passions and excluded the compromise. Perhaps, as I am tempted to believe, it is the very nature of industrialized warfare which ends by com-

municating hatred and fury to the masses and inspiring statesmen with the desire to disrupt the map of the old continent. The fact is that the first war of the century illustrates the transition toward the absolute form of a war whose political stake the belligerents are incapable of specifying.[11]

The new situation called for new ideas and new institutions. The nineteenth-century diplomatic world of The Hague seemed quaint in its legalism—and in the confidence that law could be elaborated other than as the expression of political purposes and an existing political status of forces. National and international politics, moreover, had blurred together. Relations between states must be understood in political terms, in a world in which political interests conflicted sharply, and in which domestic political life and commercial interests spilled over easily into international conflict. International law was no longer the framework for diplomacy—it could be a tool, but no more.

Those interested in maintaining international peace and order needed political science, and the new science of "international relations" to study the "systems" of international order—balance of power, bipolarity, and so on—rather than the legal boundaries and perquisites of sovereign authority. Specialists in international relations rethought the history of eighteenth- and nineteenth-century international stability in the key of diplomatic history rather than law, as a function of a scientifically discernable political "order" among states (usually the "balance of power"), rather than as the product of a shared elite consensus about the legitimate and legal limits of sovereign aspiration. Commentators today often conflate Elihu Root's enthusiasm for international legal arbitration with Wilson's enthusiasm for the League of Nations. At the time, they were opposed visions—indeed, Root, founder of the American Society of International Law, was a leader in the Republican fight against ratification of the League Covenant. He did so not in the name of American isolationism, but to support an alternative, legal order of rules and arbitration, rather than what he saw as the political entanglement of membership in a standing international organization. Wilson had been a professor of political science.

No sooner had political scientists interred the world of legal restraint in the name of a new realism about the inevitability of interstate conflict and the revolutionary force of war, than they reimagined the nature of international stability. Where such international order as had been achieved in the eighteenth and nineteenth centuries had been the product of the invisible hand of the "balance of power system," that system had reached its limit when revolutionary efforts to remake the international order were sparked by the passions of local and national politics. Domestic political passions, particularly the claims of national minorities within states, now had the power to transform international relations. The old balance of power diplomacy among sovereign states could not manage politics that put in question the states themselves.

A new diplomacy would be needed to *manage* these claims, allow room for the peaceful transformation of the international order, and harness the collective interest in avoiding global war to enforce the authority of global institutions to serve as the terrain for the sensible management of international conflict. Organizations—like the League or the International Labor Organization—would respond to common problems and harness the instruments of war to the interests of peaceful change and global stability. War could be avoided and limited not through respect for the classical legal order, but through the emergence of a new, more realistic institutional order to manage national interests *and* national passions, ensuring both stability and a process for "peaceful change."[12]

The post–World War I generation found the origins for this new regime of peace in their experience of war. Wartime necessities forced the allies to cooperate, rendering plausible the idea that war could be managed. Harold Nicolson described what he had learned from the experience of technical wartime cooperation and management in these terms:

> In the place of a national policy expressing itself by competitive and conflicting diplomacy, you had a common international interest imposing the need of international cooperation. Nor was this the only difference. Instead of national policy trying to impose itself from above upon the facts of a situation you had a system by which the facts imposed themselves upon a policy.[13]

The great interwar theorist and historian of international organization Alfred Zimmern traced the League directly to the "Allied war-machine."

> This small body [the Allied Maritime Transport Executive] was the hub of the Allied war-machine. From it went forth, daily and hourly, decisions which closely affected the interests, the needs and, above all, the daily habits of individuals over a large part of the world. And here too, under the impact of experience, were being hammered out conclusions as to the possibilities and limits of interstate cooperation which could have been arrived at in no other way. It was no accident that, when . . . the Secretariat of the League of

> Nations came to be formed, three out of the four members
> of the Transport Executive . . . transferred their experience
> and driving power to its service.[14]

Peace would be managed through a continuation of the means
of war. Although Nicolson was terribly disillusioned by his experience negotiating the establishment of the League of Nations at Paris in 1919 ("We came to Paris confident that the
new order was about to be established; we left it convinced
that the new order had merely fouled the old"),[15] he remained
optimistic that from the chaos of the war a new diplomacy and
a new mode of order had been established.

> If, therefore, one concentrates upon the continuity of diplo-
> matic theory rather than upon its discontinuity, one is im-
> pressed by the fact that, in spite of the several different
> shapes which it assumed, and in spite of dramatic periods
> when violence momentarily became more authoritative
> than reason, it is possible to recognize a distinct upward
> curve of progress. What is the nature of that progress?
> I should define it as follows: "the progress of diplomatic
> theory has been from the narrow conception of exclusive
> tribal rights to the wider conception of inclusive common
> interests."[16]

The new field of international relations would remember
the nineteenth-century as a world of diplomatic history, whereas
classical international lawyers continued to remember it as a
world of doctrine. In the twentieth-century, beginning with
those who built the new world of international organizations,
law and politics would be merged in a new consensus about
the possibilities for cooperation, reinforced by the progressive

move of history from an era of sovereign autonomy to one of inevitable intersovereign cooperation. The new problems of the new century—and the specter of newly destructive possibilities of warfare—made progress toward a more cooperative international order inevitable, if only men would seize the opportunity to manage their relations in the new institutions of international public life. International lawyers working in this new spirit would move from building international organizations to rethinking classical legal doctrines and the international political order for which they hoped the new international law might become the shared language. As Louis Henkin would put it, looking back on the League late in the twentieth-century, "For the first time, nations tried to bring within the realm of law those ultimate political tensions and interests that had long been deemed beyond control of law."[17]

The most direct impact of this new institutional diplomacy was to transform thinking about the sovereign prerogative to go to war. War remained the legal prerogative of sovereigns, but the new international regime sought to transform the political context within which sovereigns would think to exercise that power. Law was primarily the instrument for building the institutions to transform the political order—not for articulating the normative boundaries and limits of sovereign power. The League would be a political institution, a standing consultative assembly of nations with a brief to facilitate peaceful settlement and peaceful change in the international political order. War would be reduced by an obligatory "cooling off" period to allow reasonable international management of conflict to step in as national passions ebbed. In Article 16 of the League Covenant, members pledged to treat an attack on any member as an act of war against all, and undertook to subject the attacking state to isolating sanctions, mobilizing and generalizing the power of the wartime alliance to defeat aggression as deterrence.

None of these efforts sought to outlaw war. The most famous—if ultimately unsuccessful—interwar effort brought statesmen together to "condemn recourse to war" and "renounce it as an instrument of national policy" in the 1928 Kellogg-Briand Pact. It was, of course, to be a short-lived renunciation. The League promise to prevent war was almost equally short-lived. But these were not the work of idealists or legalists. Their architects were disenchanted with classical legalism and thought themselves thoroughly modern and realistic in their engagement with policy and politics.

As we look back on these interwar lawyers and political scientists from the perspective of post-1945 hindsight, it is easy to disparage their efforts. We should remember that it also remains unclear whether seventeenth-century "unjust" war ideas ever really limited the use of military force. They may well have done more to delegitimate the enemy and justify the cause. Late-nineteenth-century legal doctrine—and arbitration schemes—seem to have been even less effective. Indeed, by the late nineteenth-century, international law had very little to say about the decision to go to war—a silence rooted in the assumption that war was an unrestrained prerogative of sovereign power. The right and capacity to make war was so central to the late-nineteenth-century legal definition of sovereignty that even in the twenties, we still find jurists assessing the international legal personality of the League by asking whether it has the "right" to make war.

We should understand the twentieth-century law of war as a century-long reaction against this nineteenth-century legal silence. The diplomats who made the League sought to replace legal doctrines with a political institution that could sanction and deter aggression, while providing a framework for peaceful change and the peaceful settlement of "disputes." The brave new world of institutional management was born.

After the Second World War, again in the name of political pragmatism, this scheme matured into a comprehensive constitutional system. The political institution would be replaced by a comprehensive constitutional order that fused political and ethical considerations in a common legal vocabulary. Although the League scheme had not lived up to its political promise, eventually the Allied Powers had, uniting to defeat an Axis of states bent on aggressive war and revolutionary change in the world order. This wartime alliance became the model for the United Nations system of collective security.

More importantly, international lawyers, diplomats, and humanitarian policymakers came to understand these institutional developments in the context of a revived law of war. In this view, the system of the United Nations Charter was more than a political regime of collective security—an institutional framework for diplomatic management of conflict. It was also a new legal order that inaugurated a new law of war.

War was no longer the free act of sovereign will. International lawyers no longer treated sovereigns as free political actors; the discipline split sharply from the field of political science and international relations on just this point. Sovereigns were understood to be part of an "international community," again thought to have been made necessary and inevitable by the shrinking of the globe and the increasingly destructive power of warfare itself. The constitutional fabric for that community was thought to be provided by international law. The traditional legal distinctions and definitions were not rehabilitated—quite the opposite. The new law would be flexible, functional, practical. Even the word "war" was eliminated from the phrase "law of war." This would be a "law of force" to manage interstate violence whether or not it was legally defined as "war" in the old terms.

The United Nations Charter laid out an ambitious scheme to establish an international monopoly of force. The UN Security Council would have responsibility for maintaining the peace. Members agreed, in Article 2.4, to "refrain in their international relations from the threat or use of force against the territorial integrity or political independence of any state, or in any other manner inconsistent with the Purposes of the United Nations." As originally conceived, the Charter system made any *first* use of force a "breach" of the peace—suspicious and presumptively illegal. Self-defense was permitted as a *response* to a first attack under Article 51, until the Security Council took up the matter. The Security Council could itself then authorize collective warfare to "maintain or restore international peace and security." No state could legitimately be the first to use force—collective security, alongside the peaceful settlement of disputes, became the projects of the Security Council.

Like any complex constitutional order, however, this scheme would need to be interpreted and kept up to date in a changing political world. As it turned out, the Cold War stalemate among the great powers blocked development of the Security Council's role in collective security. Alternative institutional mechanisms needed to be found. In the Korean War, the United States and its allies relied on the General Assembly for authorization. In the 1960s and 1970s, successive Secretaries-General developed new roles for the United Nations *between* the Cold War antagonists in a variety of third world conflicts. They developed new methods of coordinated diplomacy and "good offices," and promoted the insertion of UN "peacekeepers" between adversaries to maintain and monitor cease-fire arrangements. These and many other innovations needed to be imagined and defended within the terms of the Charter. To accommodate them, the Charter was interpreted—by those who used it, by elites who approved their uses of it, and sometimes by the World Court—flexibly.

The United Nations legal order prohibited war—except as authorized by the UN Charter. That is the key point: not as authorized *by the UN*, but as authorized by the Charter. Like any constitution, the Charter was drafted in broad strokes and would need to be interpreted. Over the years, what began as an effort to monopolize force has become a constitutional regime of legitimate justifications for warfare. There is no doubt that the Charter system of principles has legitimated a great deal of warfare. Numerous governments initiated military action after 1945—not once, until the 1991 Gulf War, with the Security Council's authorization. International lawyers interpreted these events—supported them, opposed them—in the language of the Charter.

The "inherent right" to use military force in "individual or collective self defense" protected by Article 51 could be—and was—interpreted broadly as well as narrowly. Is an attack necessary? What about preemptive strikes? What about preventive wars? A close reading of Article 2.4 revealed other loopholes—force not directed "against a state," not "inconsistent with the Purposes of the United Nations." The Charter came to be read as a constitutional document articulating the legitimate justifications for warfare. Lengthy articles and books were written parsing the meaning of "aggression" and "intervention." Does economic pressure count? The conventional levers of diplomacy—the routine arrangements of commercial life—suddenly seemed arrayed on a continuum with invasion. At the same time, it was hard to think of a use of force that *could not* be legitimated in the Charter's terms. It is a rare statesman who launches a war simply to *be aggressive*. There is almost always something else to be said—the province is actually ours, our rights have been violated, our enemy is not, in fact, a state, we were invited to help, they were about to attack us, we are promoting the purposes and principles of the United Nations. Something.

This modern vocabulary of force has a jurisprudence—an attitude about the relationship between law and power. It is the flexible jurisprudence of principles and policies—of balancing conflicting considerations—familiar from many domestic constitutional systems. Legal scholar Oscar Schachter gave perhaps the best description in his eulogy for Dag Hammarskjöld— who epitomized the new jurisprudential spirit.

> Hammarskjold made no sharp distinction between law and policy; in this he departed clearly from the prevailing positivist approach. He viewed the body of law not merely as a technical set of rules and procedures, but as the authoritative expression of principles that determine the goals and directions of collective action. . . . It is also of significance in evaluating Hammarskjold's flexibility that he characteristically expressed basic principles in terms of opposing tendencies (applying, one might say, the philosophic concept of polarity or dialectical opposition). He never lost sight of the fact that a principle, such as that of observance of human rights, was balanced by the concept of nonintervention, or that the notion of equality of states had to be considered in a context which included the special responsibilities of the Great Powers. The fact that such precepts had contradictory implications meant that they could

not provide automatic answers to particular problems, but rather that they served as criteria which had to be weighed and balanced in order to achieve a rational solution of the particular problem. . . . He did not, therefore, attempt to set law against power. He sought rather to find within the limits of power the elements of common interest on the basis of which joint action and agreed standards could be established.[18]

The difficulty, of course, is the old question, "Who decides?" The signature theme for this modern vocabulary of force was *realism*—about war, about sovereign power, about politics. For all the common institutional machinery, in the first instance, every sovereign would remain judge of its own case. Leo Gross termed the process "auto-interpretation." But auto-interpretation was the beginning, not the end of the matter. In the international order, constitutional law obligations would not be decided by a supreme court. Rather, the judicial "function," cut loose from any particular institution, would come to be exercised by the global elites to whom sovereigns would make the case for their desired interpretation of Charter obligations. The Charter scheme would be interpreted collectively by the "international community" of diplomats, government officials, legal professionals (Oscar Schachter famously termed them the "college of international lawyers") and media commentators reacting to assertions of sovereign prerogative.[19]

This new decentralized judicial conception of the dialogue among international elites encouraged a conception of the Charter vocabulary as more than a set of legal commitments or political arrangements. To speak of war—or peace—in these terms was to invoke a broader ethical commitment to the existence of an "international community," rejecting both the naked power and formal law of the nineteenth-century. The United Nations joined hands with nongovernmental institutions to mobilize the public opinion of the world's elites behind humanitarian commitments through inspections, reports, inquiries, and the politics of shame. The Charter offered a vocabulary for speaking ethically about making war. It was not surprising to find the law of force increasingly expressed in the language of criminal justice—war crimes, war criminals— and in the language of human rights. To reject the language of the United Nations as the discourse of war was to defy the international community, the world—civilization itself. You can argue whatever you like, but within the constraints of this common language of civilization.

This constitutionalization of the law of force had an impact on the formal distinctions of the traditional law of war. Once the use of force has become the expression of the constitutional decisions of the international community as a whole, whether through the Security Council or otherwise, the idea of remaining "neutral" seems altogether less benign; it may even be legally inconceivable. Either you are part of the international community or you are not. It is not surprising to find this vocabulary used by an ever wider array of people to discuss the restraint and exercise of military power by statesmen, military strategists, and humanitarians alike. In the last decades, indeed, these groups have all come to speak in terms of the new law of force. It would be tempting to say that the new law of force has captured war in a legal vocabulary: war must now be legally justified, force has been linked to the exercise of rights, and the Security Council has established a monopoly on the power to judge and enforce sovereign rights. Some international lawyers have interpreted the Charter in this way. But only some. One could also say the law had been captured by politics, rendered soft and pliable by well-meaning people whose efforts to make the law stronger had only rendered it incapable of distinguishing war from peace. In the end, it is difficult to imagine even these differences of opinion about the nature of international law and the international political process being ironed out in any way other than through an open-ended political/legal/ethical conversation.

Legal Realism and the Transformation of the Law in War

The twentieth-century merger of politics, ethics, and law in a new "law of force" was accompanied by parallel changes in the nineteenth-century "law in war" rules about weaponry, prisoners, and behavior on the battlefield. The modern law in war is known to the Red Cross and to much of the European international law establishment as "humanitarian law." The U.S. military calls it the "law of armed conflict." They are speaking about the same thing. I prefer the classic term "law in war," or *jus in bello.*

In its traditional form, the law in war relied heavily on the distinctions of nineteenth-century law—between peace and war, public and private actors, civilians and combatants. It is easy to see how the boundaries of classical international law could be transformed into humanitarian limits on sovereign behavior in wartime: combatants must respect the inviolability of civilians, belligerents of neutrals, and so forth. The law in war—codified in successive waves from the 1899 Hague Declarations on asphyxiating gases and expanding bullets, through the 1907 Hague Conventions on the "rights and duties of neutral powers" and the "laws and customs of war" on land

and at sea, to the 1949 Geneva Conventions on treatment of
the wounded and sick "in the Field" and of prisoners of war
and civilians "in time of war"—trades heavily in these distinctions. Only the more recent codifications of the 1970s and
1980s blur the line between international and noninternational "armed conflicts," reaching out to all the "victims" of conflict, or mandating measures to avoid environmental damage
whether on or off the battlefield.

The story of the transformation of the Hague/Geneva rule
system into a modern vocabulary of political legitimacy can
best be told against the background of a widespread twentieth-
century loss of faith in the formal distinctions of classical legal
thought—in the wisdom, as well as the plausibility and usefulness, of separating law sharply from politics, or private right
sharply from public power, or, for that matter, war from peace,
civilian from combatant.

The traditional law in war was not only the product of these
distinctions. Those who codified the law at the Hague and
Geneva did more than deduce limits on warfare from the nature
of sovereignty or the boundaries of sovereign public authority in
war. Early humanitarian law relied on these background distinctions of classical international law, but the rules were more detailed: How could you distinguish combatants from civilians?
What treatment should be accorded those who placed themselves outside the battlefield? Humanitarians reacting to the violence of nineteenth-century warfare in the Crimea and in the
American Civil War worked with military authorities to develop
these more detailed codes of conduct. Often these were promulgated in national regulations; sometimes they were also negotiated among sovereigns and promulgated by treaty.

The goal was to get military professionals to hammer out
workable rules, on the theory that they could be expected to

respect rules they had generated and to which their states had consented. As a humanitarian strategy, this approach relied on the internal professional disciplinary structures of the military. From the start, the law in war, like the International Committee of the Red Cross with which it is prominently associated, has prided itself on its pragmatic relationship with military professionals. Despite their rather different professional cultures, military lawyers and lawyers from the Red Cross are often able to find common ground with surprising ease. They attend the same conferences and speak the same language, though they may differ on this or that interpretation or detail.

Developing a insider vocabulary common to humanitarian and military professionals was intended to place the new rules on a firm footing in the militarily plausible. No exploding bullets. Safe passage for ambulances and medical personnel wearing identifiable outfits, and so forth. To this day, the most significant codifications of the law in war have indeed been negotiated among diplomatic and military authorities. The idea, moreover, was that soldiers on both sides of a conflict had a shared professional interest in more humane rules of conduct. It is not surprisingly that Francis Lieber, author of an early military code of conduct, had relatives on both sides in our Civil War.

Moreover, to preserve its public neutrality and maintain the confidence of national military leaders, the ICRC has traditionally reported only to governments and only on the basis of confidentiality. It has been more comfortable monitoring compliance with these precise negotiated rules than interpreting broad standards, although, as we have seen, a great deal of ink can be spilled over the precise definition of a legal term such as "torture" or "inhumane and degrading punishment."

This strategy had obvious drawbacks: reliance on military acquiescence limited what could be achieved. Narrowly drawn rules permit a great deal and legitimate what is permitted. Military leaders outlaw weapons that they no longer need, or against which defense would be too expensive or difficult, or that they feel will be potent tools only for their adversaries. Indeed, it rarely turns out to be true that clear rules will affect forces on both sides of a conflict the same way, for much will depend upon their resources, tactics, and strategy. Recognition of these costs is one reason the modern pragmatism of the law in war has always meant more than the deference to sovereign consent we associate with nineteenth-century positivism. Humanitarians seeking to develop a practical and workable limit on the violence of warfare have not been content to stop with the clear rules they could induce military authorities to accept.

Humanitarian pragmatism has also brought a deeper set of changes to the nineteenth-century law in war. The clear distinctions that provided the background for so many of the more detailed rules lost their luster. The rules themselves were transformed into—or even replaced by—broad principles and standards. Most importantly, the modern humanitarian and military professionals have come to think about the status of the law itself in new ways—less as an external or ex post judge of military behavior than as a vocabulary for arguing about the legitimacy and illegitimacy of military conduct common to those inside and outside the military profession.

The nineteenth-century legal distinctions that formed the background for many of the more detailed rules themselves came under pressure in several ways. In political terms, they seemed associated with a view of the international world that placed too much emphasis on the autonomy of sovereigns, and not enough on the necessity for cooperation in an "international community." When international lawyers reasoned about what sovereigns could and could not do by deduction from the legal nature of sovereignty, moreover, their arguments no longer seemed persuasive. Sovereignty could mean something else, and the old international law had little to say about what it *should* mean. The absolute on/off nature of the nineteenth-century distinctions—either it was war or it was peace—seemed far too rigid to facilitate the more nuanced approach to diplomacy opened up by unbundling sovereignty into a collection of competences, and arranging diplomatic efforts to influence other sovereigns along a continuum from diplomatic suggestion to invasion.

At the same time, the nineteenth-century rules and sharp distinctions were joined in the twentieth-century by broader standards and loose criteria for judgment. The formal distinction between combatants and noncombatants became a "principle of distinction" between military and nonmilitary objectives. The rules developed since the 1860s are now presented as having ripened into customary obligations, if not in their details, at least in their broad outlines. As customary law, they can be boiled down to a few broad commitments. The detailed rules originally agreed at The Hague or Geneva about whom one can target and how civilians, medical personnel, the wounded, or prisoners of war must be treated have morphed into standards, simple ideas that can be printed on a wallet-sized card and taught easily to soldiers in the field. "The means of war are not unlimited"; "each use of force must be necessary" and "proportional"—these have become ethical baselines for a universal modern civilization.

Humanitarians have sought to turn rules into principles to generalize the narrow achievements of negotiation, transforming narrow treaties into broad custom. This has been a particularly attractive strategy for human rights activists and others far outside the military profession. Speaking publicly in international settings, they have sought to shame governments into compliance and have always been more at ease than Red Cross professionals framing arguments in broad standards. But military professionals have also turned to standards, to ease training through simplification, to emphasize the importance of *judgment* by soldiers and commanders operating under the rules, or simply to cover situations not included under the formal rules with a consistent practice. For example, a standard Canadian military manual instructs that the "spirit and principles" of the international law of armed conflict apply to noninternational conflicts not covered by the terms of the agreed rules.[20]

At the same time, we should not exaggerate the move from rules to standards. The nineteenth-century law in war was also filled with broad propositions about sovereign prerogatives and the entailments of the status of neutral or belligerent, or the nature of combat, while the technical rules of humanitarian law, and the most technical disarmament treaties, were negotiated in the twentieth-century. We also find military lawyers turning broad principles and nuanced judgments into simple bright-line rules of engagement for soldiers in combat, while humanitarians have combed military handbooks and government statements of principle that were promulgated for all sorts of purposes to distill "rules" of customary international law. The ICRC's recent three-volume restatement of the customary law of armed conflict is a monumental work of advocacy of just this type.

The tendency to focus on standards when describing the modern law in war is the consequence of a broader shift in ideas about the significance and usefulness of the law in war as a whole. Foregrounding standards like "proportionality" or "military necessity" presents the law in war simultaneously as a broad ethical discourse and as a framework for judgment capable of making the cost-benefit calculations necessary for it to be a useful tool for military professionals. The classic distinctions—between belligerent and neutral, or civilian and combatant—are still there, but their status has been transformed. They *may* be useful benchmarks for the humanitarian limits of warfare—but they may not be.

If we think about things from an ethical point of view, we may sometimes conclude that it is, in fact, more humanitarian to kill civilians to save soldiers. Think Hiroshima. Or that it may be more humanitarian to intervene than to respect territorial sovereignty. Think Rwanda, Armenia, Cambodia, or the Holocaust. The transformation of formal distinctions into benchmarks that might or might not be persuasive in a particular context also makes every distinction a matter of more or less.

Of course, humanitarians and military professionals might well do the evaluation differently. Nevertheless, an antiformal law in war of broad standards represents a triumph for grasping the nettle of costs and benefits. In debating whether this or that is, in fact, proportional or necessary, moreover, humanitarians and military professionals are at least speaking the same language. As they argue, it would not be difficult for humanitarians to conclude that they had infiltrated the background decision-making of those whom they would bend to humanitarian ends. Nor would it be surprising if military professionals experienced their professional calculations as expressions of their own humanity.

Either way, as a framework for debate and judgment, this new law in war embraces the unavoidability of trade-offs, of balancing harms, of accepting costs to achieve benefit—an experience common to both military strategists and humanitarians. Take civilian casualties. Of course, civilians *will* be killed in war. Limiting civilian death has become a pragmatic commitment—no *unnecessary* damage, not one more civilian than necessary. In the vernacular of humanitarian law, no "superfluous injury," and no "unnecessary suffering." The range of complex strategic calculations opened up by this idea—for those inside and outside the military—is broad indeed. We might say that the old distinction between combatants and civilians has been relativized.

Of course, it is but a short step from here to "effects-based targeting"—and the elimination of the doctrinal firewall between civilian and military, belligerent and neutral. I was struck during the NATO bombardment of Belgrade—justified by the international community's humanitarian objectives in Kosovo—by the public discussions among military strategists *and* humanitarian international lawyers of the appropriateness of targeting the civilian elites most strongly supporting the Milošević regime. If bombing the bourgeoisie would have been more effective than a long march inland toward the capital, would it have been proportional, necessary—humanitarian—to place the war's burden on young draftees in the field rather than upon the civilian population who sent them there? Some argued that targeting civilians supporting an outlaw—if democratic—regime would also extend the Nuremberg principle of individual responsibility. Others disagreed, of course. But the terms of their disagreement were provided by shared principles. Thinking in humanitarian terms, why *shouldn't* military operations be judged by their effects, rather than by their adherence to narrow rules that might well have all manner of perverse and unpredictable outcomes?

At the same time, the modern law in war represents a transformation in our sense for what it means to say that something is or is not "legal." The classical period bequeathed a professional tendency to think of the legal order as a neutral and external framework for policing the boundaries between legitimate and illegitimate uses of force. When legal elites think in this classical register—as they often certainly still do—they place the emphasis on the *validity* of norms. Something is legal if it complies with a valid norm. A norm is valid if it was promulgated by the appropriate authority using the authorized procedure, or if it can be deduced from first principles by recognized professional canons of deduction and interpretation. If the norm is valid, it should be followed. In the world of validity, the law is the law—you should follow it because it is valid. If what you did on the battlefield was not precluded by a valid prohibition, you remain privileged to kill. Full stop. If you violate the laws in war, you can be court-martialed.

This idea makes a lot of intuitive sense in a vertical national legal order, where we picture a court and a police force in the background determining which norms are valid and enforcing them. In the twentieth century, jurists tried to extend this model to the international arena by building functional substitutes for courts and policemen. This might mean relying on national courts, or internal military discipline to enforce the valid rules. Or building a world court. But once you begin thinking of the international legal order as backstopped by a "court of public opinion," or international norms being enforced through the decentralized process through which the "international community" makes the political initiatives of those who are perceived to break the norms less legitimate and therefore more costly to undertake, the idea of "validity" makes less sense. There is no authoritative determiner of the norms and interpretations that are, in fact, *valid.* That may not be so much of a problem if the rules are clear or where elites agree about what they mean, but once we start foregrounding broad standards like "proportional" or "necessary" about which increasingly diverse participants in the broad conversation that is the global political process will disagree, that will be more complicated.

As a result, an alternative way of thinking about the status—and enforceability—of norms has developed which emphasizes the *persuasiveness,* rather than the validity of norms. In this way of thinking, you should follow the norms because you are persuaded you should. You might be persuaded because you believe the norm is valid and think you should follow the valid rules. But you might also be persuaded because you think the rule is wise or ethically compelling. Or because you think it encapsulates best practice. Or because you fear the consequences of not following it. Or for some other reason. This way of thinking is not altogether new—it harks back, in a sense, to Vattel's elaboration of rules as wise counsel for statesmen in a common legal/moral/political order. You declare war because you want to give the other side the opportunity to knuckle under without killing anybody if you can—because you want to take advantage of the communicative power of an army massed on the border.

As in Vattel's day, this mode of thinking is only plausible if one imagines that everyone in the system is participating in the same normative universe, if adversaries speak, in fact, the same language. Where there are revolutionary powers or outsiders to the global civilization, it doesn't work—but then, neither do the *valid* norms. The astonishing thing is the extent to which those on all sides of even the most asymmetric postcolonial conflicts do, in fact, speak the same language. In the meantime, however, part of that language is the assertion that one's adversary is, in fact, outside the fabric of a common civilization.

Once elites began thinking about international norms in this way, it was a short step to the idea that a norm was valid law only if it turned out, in fact, to *have been* persuasive. The point about a norm is not its pedigree, but its persuasiveness. The more persuasive norms have more of an effect—and only those norms that have an effect should rightly be considered "legal." In this framework, statements about one's entitlements—or an adversary's crimes and misdemeanors—are assertions, hypotheses, wagers on how the community of relevant interpreters will react. If they accept the proposition, the entitlement is valid, the violation a crime. If they don't, they aren't. Whether the argument was, in any event, a plausible one is a matter of professional ethics. Was the lawsuit "altogether frivolous" or simply a loser?

We might understand the American assertion that those held at Guantanamo were in a new, limbo legal status as "illegal combatants" in this way. It was a terminological innovation that seemed to place those captured in a legal no-man's-land, neither criminals entitled to legal defense, nor prisoners of war entitled to the treatment prescribed by the law in war. The doctrinal category of "unprivileged combatants" had been around since the nineteenth-century, to refer to those who commit hostilities without being part of an organized and hostile armed force.[21] Once the sharp line between war and peace, armed conflict and other hostile acts had been softened by the move to a twentieth-century law of force, one might have supposed that all those engaged in hostile acts, whether strictly speaking part of a hostile army, would be covered by the rules governing more formally recognized combatants. Or, one might have supposed that all those not easily classifiable as members of a foreign army, once captured, would be treated as civilian criminals.

The U.S. administration tried something else, redeploying the old category in a way that made its use seem the product of their strategy. If you want to interrogate them and you don't want a lawyer present, you need to get them out of the category of either criminal defendant or prisoner of war. So, "unlawful combatant." But this is only the first step. To many elites, this American claim seemed plausible—there were the doctrinal precedents, and the presumed background intention to interrogate those who had been captured seemed altogether sensible. But to other elites, it did not seem plausible at all. The doctrinal category seemed to have gone out with the nineteenth-century—and with good reason. The point now was to treat everyone humanely and legally, either as a criminal or a prisoner of war. The American assertion seemed, in a sense, too much the product of their instrumental objective, too self-serving. To the extent the doctrine was in fact unclear, there were also political considerations of image—did this send the message of toughness, or of overreaching by a great power? Was it more important to err on the side of doctrinal compliance or of vigorous defense of democratic civilization itself?

The story has not ended. The pebble of American assertion has dropped in the pond, and it may be many years and many conflicts before we can evaluate its effects. Surely the assertion emboldened some in the administration, but other allies may well have become disaffected. The will of the enemy may well have been strengthened—and weakened. Some of those who interpreted the situation differently from the administration will have had some power to persuade those with the ability to bring costs to bear on the American administration to do so—

U.S. courts, foreign media commentators, military lawyers, human rights organizations, allied governments—by objecting and interpreting the situation differently.

Who is right? Contemporary international lawyers may each have their own opinion about that, but ultimately the proof will be in the pudding. How will the American assertion play out in the international political process? Will others in similar situations copy the American approach or shy away from it. Will the Americans give it up? Will they hold to the assertion, but simply not try it again to avoid facing the same resistance? It is likely the result will not be clear: the opposition will have *some* force, as will the assertion. To speak realistically about the law—and to advise a client in the next case—we would need to treat the normative proposition itself as *somewhat* persuasive. Reimagined as tools of persuasion, the validity or bindingness or force of norms becomes itself a matter of more or less. Some arguments will, of course, persuade no one; they will be considered completely frivolous, outside the professional consensus about what it is plausible to argue. But the most useful legal—and political—advice will include an assessment of the likely *impact* of a normative assertion.

This idea has a long history in legal thought. In the American tradition, it stretches back at least to Oliver Wendell Holmes. For Holmes, law was not a mystery, still less an abstract system or science—it was a profession. Law was what law did. It was Holmes to insisted that "the prophecies of what the courts will do in fact, and nothing more pretentious, are what I mean by the law."[22] It was no use talking about "rights" in the abstract; what mattered were remedies. If there was no remedy, no court to enforce the norm, it was not meaningful to speak of the norm as "law." The point is not law in the books, it is law in action, as it looked from the perspective of a person who might seek to violate it.

In the court of world public opinion, the laws in force are not necessarily the rules that are *valid*, in some technical sense, but the rules that are persuasive to relevant political constituencies. Whether a norm is or is not legal is a function not of its origin or pedigree, but of its effects. Law has an effect—is law—when it *persuades* an audience with political clout that something someone else did, or plans to do, is or is not legitimate. The point is no longer the validity of distinctions, but the persuasiveness of arguments.

This change in perspective also affected the law in war. For humanitarians, the point was to develop norms that would be persuasive. This might be done by getting the military to agree to them. But it might be done in other ways as well, by blending familiar distinctions (civilian/combatant) with broader ethical considerations. When the International Committee of the Red Cross completed its lengthy restatement of the rules and standards of the customary international law in war, it was written entirely in the key of validity: here is a definitive statement of the rules that we have determined, after careful scientific inquiry, to be valid. But it is not surprising that many of the interpretations have been seen by others to be tendentious readings, advancing the Red Cross agenda. States that have persistently opposed interpretations included in the Red Cross restatement—including the United States—have protested their validity in classic terms: we did not consent. At the same time, there is no gainsaying the likely *persuasiveness* of the Red Cross statements in many contexts and to many audiences. It was with this in mind that humanitarian foundations underwrote the lengthy Red Cross restatement process; the whole point was to strengthen, develop, advance humanitarian law. To persuade—to offer a new platform, a new floor, for discussions of the persuasive limits to force in war.

We also now understand that such an effort to persuade can be either enhanced, or undermined, by the presentation of the restatement in the rhetoric of validity. If the rules can be shown to be invalid, their persuasiveness may crumble. If presented as ethical standards or as pragmatic methods to achieve a common objective, they may well be more persuasive. But not to an audience fixated on whether or not the rules are valid. The fact that the modern law in war is expressed in the keys of both validity and persuasion makes the professional use of its vocabulary by both humanitarian and military professionals a complex challenge.

Both humanitarian and military professionals are used to working with the law of armed conflict in the key of validity. They make rules by careful negotiation. They influence customary rules by intentioned and public behavior. The military sends ships through straits or close to shorelines both to assert and to strengthen rights. Both professions will need to become more adept at operations in the law of persuasion, the domain in which the image of a single dead civilian can make out a persuasive case for violation that trumps the most ponderous technical legal defense, the domain in which the ICRC restates the law *as advocacy.*

The law in war *of persuasion* is not only the product of overreaching humanitarian outsiders, of course. The military also interprets, advocates—seeks to persuade. This key point is that the modernization of the law in war has transformed it into a vocabulary for assessing military conduct in war that merges what once were autonomous legal distinctions, ethical principles, and pragmatic military calculations—and placed them all in the service of a broad political process through which the legitimacy and illegitimacy of military conduct is assessed. This opens opportunities for humanitarians and military professionals alike—but also new dangers.

3 ✣ War by Law

Warfare today takes place in a political and legal context that draws on each phase in the history I have been tracing. Little has been lost. Military action is routinely challenged—and defended—in a rhetoric of "just war" that is hundreds of years old, updated by modern political theories of justice and ethical or religious theories of virtue. The sharp distinctions of nineteenth-century legal thought, confidence in the convergence of legitimate interests, and in the peaceful effects of an expanding global economic and commercial system structured by private ordering, remain vivid in the minds and discourse of international elites considering the legitimacy of warfare. Sixteenth-, seventeenth-, eighteenth-, and nineteenth-century ideas are all still to be found, as arguments which sometimes persuade. They have been joined by innovative twentieth-century ways of speaking about the legitimacy of using force— new rules, new principles, and reinterpretations of the earlier traditions.

It is hard to understand the modern law of commercial life except as a lived practice, a fluid terrain pushed and pulled by businessmen, regulators, financiers, employees, consumers, and more. The modern law about war is similar. For military and humanitarian professionals alike, the historical sediment of arguments and institutions offers strategic opportunities and limitations—it is there to be used, respected, and remade. Humanitarian and military professionals making war and peace with the norms, institutions, and language of modern law may be more or less skilled, successful, or strategic. Their arguments and assertions and tactics may be persuasive, or altogether too clever. In corporate practice, you encounter businessmen who are better or worse at getting the most from their attorneys. Some are adept at using law strategically, treating contracts as tools for planning and communicating, as well as binding their commercial partners. For others, law is just something they bump into when they haven't been paying attention. I hope this book contributes to a more strategic sensibility about the law among military and humanitarian professionals. At the same time, waging war by law can do real damage, blunting the human experience of responsibility for the violence and havoc wrought by our professional decisions.

Battle in the Shadow of Sharp Distinctions and Outsider Ethics: Traces of the Premodern Legal Order

The ethical language of early just war thinking, coupled with the sharp boundaries of the classical nineteenth-century laws about sovereignty, is a mixed legacy for humanitarian and military professionals alike. Traces of the idea that sovereigns have uniquely autonomous and absolute powers in the field of war continue to embolden national leaders, although we can see how easy it is underestimate the complex diplomatic and

legal—as well as military—terrain on which the war will need
to be fought and won. Just war ideas can bolster the leadership, just as they must have done in the sixteenth century.
Making war to fulfill the purposes of the United Nations
Charter, promote democracy, or defend human rights must
feel different from battling for crude oil or crass political advantage. It is hard to predict the impact of just war ideas on
the violence of warfare once things get going. Wedding war to
justice might well open the door to humanist limitations on
the use of force. The proselytizing spirit Vitoria encouraged in
the Spanish conquistadors did place the Indians in the same
universal moral order, if it also justified their slaughter. It is
difficult in our modern era to know whether more—or less—
violence would be justified in warfare for a just cause. If proportionality is the test, we might well conclude that more
civilians could be slaughtered to stop a holocaust than in a
routine effort to defend one's territory. It is difficult to know.

It is easy, moreover, to see the opportunities for humanitarian advocacy opened by the continued existence of a vocabulary of legal validity, sharp distinctions, and outsider virtue.
When advocates today deploy the classical vocabulary of the
nineteenth-century law of war, they can seem—to themselves,
to their audience—to bring an external reason to bear on the
violence of war and an external ethical passion to bear on the
cold calculation that war sometimes makes sense. I have a
great deal of sympathy for this humanitarian tradition, forged
in the nineteenth-century separation of juridical thought from
the politics and public policy of warfare. It is where my own
professional and ethical journey began—in a moral world for
which the Clausewitzian perspective was precisely the problem. To think war and peace continuous was to think the un-
thinkable, and to flirt with a cynical, real-political point of

view that, because it could think war, might also find itself
making war. Only those who could tell the difference between
war and peace, clearly, definitively, seemed to have any hope of
limiting war's violence.

We should remember, however, that the military professional also benefited from the nineteenth-century structure of
clear norms marking virtue from vice and regulating the battlefield as a space marked off from civilian or commercial routine. Of course, in the nineteenth century, these sharp boundaries were built around an image of sovereign authority to
make war that was itself unrestrained. But even restrained by
the clear requirements of justice, a sovereign military power
and a battlefield sharply differentiated from the civilian world
of peace have powerful advantages. Most directly, the classic
law established a privilege to kill on the battlefield; what
would otherwise be murder was now legally privileged and legitimate.[1] Military professionals the world over are emboldened by the confidence that what they do on the battlefield, in
war, should be judged by different standards, tested by different rules, than what they do at home with their families, when
their communities are at peace.

Moreover, a sharp separation between the law of war, regulating the justice of declaring war in the first place, and the law
in war, regulating conduct on the battlefield, separates the responsibility of political leaders—the sovereign—from that of
the military. It becomes reasonable for the military professional to feel that the justice of war is simply not his or her
responsibility. That belongs to the civilian elites—the politicians, the sovereign. For the military, legitimacy and virtue are
measured by the law in war alone. Something similar can happen at the political level, where it is easy to feel that whatever
violence is done on the battlefield is the responsibility of one's

military commanders, checked by the law in war. If the cause is just, the war legitimate, responsibility for the violence wrought by its execution compels us only to understand and support our troops. Whatever the virtues of citizen control over the military, there remains something odd about distinguishing the civilian and military professions in such a way that no one need feel responsible for both making war and killing people.

Ultimately, political and military professionals responsible for warfare would find the nineteenth-century legal regime insufficiently flexible for making—and resisting—modern warfare. Nevertheless, the traditional law continues to be useful to cabin and channel the effort, discipline the troops, and preserve the boundaries of professional expertise and responsibility. The law of sharp distinctions can still facilitate the identification of appropriate targets, or prevent the enemy's civilian resources from blurring into the war effort. It can define and delegitimate enemy perfidy. It is easy, moreover, to understand the military's attachment to universally accepted rules about the treatment of the wounded, or prisoners, or those outside the battlefield—they might well find themselves wounded or captured. The classic law continues to express—and channel—ethical sensibility. There may be no military reason for wanton violence, but human sentiment also calls out for humane treatment when one is no longer able to pursue the professional mission to destroy the enemy. In some strange way, the medic who treats the fallen enemy alongside his comrade in arms ennobles the whole project—makes it seem reasonable, somehow, to have shot the guy in the first place.

For humanitarians, the law of sharp distinctions can blunt the practice of more nuanced judgment about the ethics of military violence. The discourse of ethical denunciation often has a tip-of-the-iceberg problem. Take Abu Ghraib—sexually humiliating, even torturing and killing prisoners is probably not, ethically speaking, the worst or most shocking thing our coalition has done in Iraq. Humanitarians are right to worry that outrage at the photos may also be a way of not thinking about other injuries, deaths, and mutilations our government has wrought.

We know, moreover, that following absolute ethical precepts in wartime—as any other time—can be taken too far and become its own idolatry. Is it sensible to clear the cave with a firebomb because tear gas, lawful when policing, is unlawful in "combat?"[2] Absolute rules lead us to imagine we know what violence is just, what unjust, always and for everyone. But justice is not like that—it must be imagined, built by people, struggled for, redefined, in each conflict in new ways. Justice requires leadership—on the battlefield and off.

For humanitarians, the strategic problem with the law of firm distinctions was that it kept the peacemakers out of the war room. The decision to make war was the unrestrained political prerogative of the sovereign; decisions about tactics of warfare were the privilege of the military profession, limited only by the external boundaries of war itself, beyond which were civilians, noncombatants, those "outside" combat. Only by breaking down the barrier, working with the military to develop common standards of behavior, could humanitarians enter debates about tactics, and subject the exercise of military privilege to standards of review—proportionality, necessity, and so forth.

Although humanitarians may be tempted by the presumption that they stand outside the military profession, that their standards are higher, their rules stricter, the appeal of an outsider posture—and the promise of clear rules—can be deceiv-

ing. In some instances, the modern military's own internal
rules of engagement are stricter than what the traditional law
in war requires. In the last years, moreover, we have seen military professionals among those most disturbed by the Bush administration's efforts to shrink or skirt humanitarian standards
in their war on terror. Has the military gone soft? Become less
willing than their civilian masters to condone harsh tactics? Or
is the scandal rather that the JAG corps was for a long time far
stronger in their opposition to harsh tactics than civilian hu-
manists who stood outside, wringing their hands, but uncertain whether they were in fact qualified to judge? Perhaps the
scandal is our sense that to torture or not to torture has become a professional judgment in the first place, unavoidably
linked to the question of whether harsh treatment will work.

The strength and significance of the military's own culture
of discipline can be difficult for civilians to grasp. It is part bureaucratic necessity, central to the effectiveness of the mission
and to the safety of colleagues. It is also as much passion as
reason—instrumentalism wrapped in honor, integrity, in a
culture set off from civilian life, a higher calling. As a social
production, military discipline is of course also, and perhaps
more importantly, a work on the self. The United States Army
runs recruitment commercials that implore, "See your re-
cruiter, become an army of one." The promise is power, to be
sure. But also discipline—self-discipline. If you join, you will
be transformed inside—*you* will become an army, coordinated,
disciplined, your own commanding officer, your own platoon,
embodying within yourself the force of hundreds because of
the work you will do, and we will do, on you.

Of course, there is opportunity for individual judgment,
error—and atrocity. Sometimes soldiers do run amok. There
are bad apples. We remember the pilots who flew beneath the

Italian ski-lift, slicing the cables. Or the precision guided missile fired in Kosovo with the tail fins put on backwards—spinning ever further from its programmed target until it exploded in a crowded civilian marketplace. The American pilots who bombed their Canadian allies. Or, for that matter, My Lai, the abuse of prisoners in Baghdad, and all the other tales of atrocity in war. Each of these circumstances is, of course, legally—and ethically—distinct. What can be hard for civilians to grasp about such situations is that soldiers tried for breach of military discipline may find that their defense is actually *stronger* under the vague standards of international humanitarian law than under their national criminal or military law. Or that international law provides the framework less for disciplining the force than for unleashing the spear at its tip.

Indeed, the international legal standards of self-defense, proportionality and necessity, are so broad that they are routinely invoked to refer to the zone of *discretion* rather than limitation. I have spoken to numerous navy pilots who describe briefings filled with technical rules of engagement and military law. After the military lawyer leaves, the commanding officer summarizes in the empowering language of international law: "Just don't do anything you don't feel is necessary, and defend yourself—don't get killed out there." The fighter pilot heads out on a leash of rules, assembled in a package coordinated by a complex transnational array of operating procedures. Only at the last moment, in contact with the enemy, is he released to the discretion framed by the law of armed conflict—necessity, self-defense.

After the Gulf War, it was widely acknowledged that the decision to take down the electrical grid by striking the generators had left power out for far longer than necessary, contributing to unsanitary water supply and the unnecessary death of many thousands from cholera. Military planners involved have admitted this was a mistake—and they have reportedly revised their procedures accordingly.[3] In Kosovo and in Iraq during the second war, such a devastating blow to the electrical grid was not struck. But in reviewing the Gulf War experience, military professionals will *not* say that taking out the generators lacked proportionality or necessity, or that it was excessive given what they knew then and what they were trying to achieve. These legal standards remain the solid ground on which their acts, and, ultimately the deaths of many thousands, can remain legitimated.

A more important doubt about a traditional law in war came from the loss of confidence that war was, in fact, so sharply distinct from peace. The pacifism that stands outside, denouncing the political/military world of war from the safe distance of ethics or legal doctrine, is difficult to square with the modern feeling that somehow the machinery of war, and calculations about life and death parallel to those made on the battlefield, have seeped into everyday life. In the twentieth century—perhaps already in our own Civil War—we learned that war is not something that happens over there, or is prosecuted only by military professionals. Our economy, our society, our culture, has been mobilized to the task—and the application of military force lies on a continuum with all manner of other powers. Opponents of the Iraq wars faced the immediate question—is the UN sanctions regime more or less humanitarian? More or less effective?

Even assuming war might be conducted "over there," in its own domain, it has become difficult to keep one's ethical distance from warfare in modern discussions of international affairs. There is the nagging problem that force also has humanitarian uses in a wicked world. Moreover, war can strengthen our moral determination; we know that great moral claims often become stronger when men and women kill and die in their name. There is some kind of feedback loop between our ethical convictions and our use of force. Moreover, we know how easily moral clarity calls forth violence and justifies warfare; it is a rare military campaign today that is not launched for some humanitarian purpose.

Looking back, this was also a great lesson of the Civil War: both parties experienced their project and excoriated their opponents as both cool reason and hot crusade. Both battled in the name of the national whole. Everyone was speaking truth to power as they went at one another tooth and nail. In the years since, we have learned how easily ethical denunciation and outrage can get us into things on which we are not able to follow through—triggering intervention in Kosovo, Afghanistan, even Iraq, with humanitarian promises on which we cannot deliver. The universal claims of human rights can seem to promise the existence of an "international community" that is simply not available to back them up.

Of course, for all these difficulties, much can sometimes be achieved by bringing humanitarian reason to bear on cultures of violence and by opposing the cruel calculations of cynical statesmen with ethical commitment. It is not clear, however, that the traditional vocabulary of clear lines and absolute ethical judgments is any longer available. For all its potential usefulness, to military and humanitarian professionals alike, in some sense the background consciousness that rendered it plausible has simply eroded. Often, the trouble begins when humanitarians speaking the language of external virtue hit the problem of exceptions—what if it were Hitler, what if there were genocide, what if they were raping your mother? What about self-defense? What about deterrence? These classic questions take us straight to the doctrinal world of flexible standards, balancing conflicting considerations, assessing proportionality, familiar to the professional weighing costs to achieve gains. To figure out when and how much self-defense is "just," we need technical, professional—military—expertise.

Some commentators reacted to the 1996 International Court of Justice opinion on the legality of the threat or use of nuclear weapons—a fabric of legal equivocations—by shaming the court for speaking with nuance about an apocalypse—for parsing the "slaughter of the innocents" into the awkward categories of the court's statute and jurisdictional rules—for worrying more about the validity of norms than the future of humanity. The horrors of warfare, the dead and mangled bodies, the lives and families ripped apart, the intense anxiety and suffering on and off the battlefield, the pain of a single wounded child crying out—it seems obscene to speak of these things in any language but that of moral clarity, regret, and outrage.

The trouble is that denouncing nuclear war as the "slaughtering the innocents" takes us directly to the definition of innocent. Placing nuclear weapons on the other side of a sharp conceptual boundary from "conventional war" is no different from sharply differentiating war from peace. What happens when the political tactics on the "good" side of the boundary seem worse? We are back to questions about the civilian elites who supported the Belgrade regime, and to issues of proportionality—how else might Japan have been defeated?

When the boundaries become unrealistic, or intuitively implausible, political and military powers will subvert them, perhaps in secret. Wouldn't it be better to bring their activities into the open? And they will burst through at unpredictable times—wouldn't a more stable peace be possible if we recognized the usefulness of these weapons, and the usefulness of war itself, placing them in a common framework for discussion? In such a discussion, we would need to account not merely for the horrors of Hiroshima and Nagasaki—but also for their singularity. How can the dangers of nuclear proliferation, nuclear error, nuclear first-use—best be prevented? For nonproliferation we need a *regime*—not a code of conduct. And the regime will need to be realistic, will need to meet the legitimate security concerns of the states that are parties, will need to secure the usefulness of nuclear energy, and so forth. A nonproliferation regime will need to take the stand-off of the nuclear powers into account, develop an attitude about the circumstances under which deterrence works and can remain stable. These are serious, difficult questions, questions of more and less, of political and legal and administrative structure.

And ultimately, the questions are no different for torture. When, if ever, does it work? When do prohibitions make it seem more potent than it is—driving it underground and into use? It is easy to imagine a regime that would make interrogation—or intimidation—more accountable, more reliable, as well as less frequent, more humane. What about requiring a warrant to torture—or judicial oversight?

This is the very difficult terrain that opens as the classic law of sharp differences fades. It offers at once new opportunities for strategy—including the strategic deployment and assertion of sharp boundaries—and the exhilarating feeling of thinking rationally about the perverse and the forbidden. Moreover, it enlists us, whether humanitarian or military professionals, as strategic actors in the drama of war. Presuming, for instance, that as humanitarian professionals, we speak about the slaughter of the innocents, or express our horror at the practice of torture, in order to reduce the likelihood of nuclear war and the incidence of torture—rather than merely to bear witness— we will need to assess ethical denunciation *itself* in tactical terms. What are the costs and benefits of denunciation? When *should* we trim our sails a bit, hold back, even flatter those whose fingers are on the button, in the name of an effective pacifism? Of course, if we hold our rhetorical fire this time, people may die. People whose death we might have prevented, in whose torture we acquiesce—whom we sacrifice for the larger ethical objective of a stronger law in war, or a more legitimate Red Cross. These are just the sorts of considerations that brought us to the modern law of armed conflict.

Modern Laws and Modern War: Problems of Strategy

The twentieth century transformed both law and war, creating a new terrain for strategy by both humanitarian and military professionals. Humanitarians helped develop a more flexible law of force as an exercise in realism. They immersed themselves in the political and military conversations they sought to influence—by infiltrating the military's own calculations with humanitarian standards, and promoting an ethically rooted vocabulary for global political discourse. Their efforts were realistic in another way as well. Warfare had changed dramatically, first in the new "world wars" of the early twentieth century, and again in the metaphoric and asymmetric wars of the postcolonial period. So had political life, becoming more global, shot through with a more malleable legal vernacular, more adept at co-opting outsider voices. It is hard to imagine how we could move back to the world of sharp boundaries and clear legal validity, however much it may sometimes appeal to us to do so. It is not just that we have lost faith in the classic distinctions between war and peace, or between civilian political decisions and their professional military implementation—faith can return. War and politics just doesn't seem like that any more.

New technologies and new modes of warfare have eroded the doctrinal world imagined in the wake of wars that seemed "modern" in the 1860s. Total war mobilized the civilian and economic worlds into war. Complex technologies, developed for commercial as well as military uses, have linked together the institutional players of war and peace. The National Security Administration and the Central Intelligence Agency rely on the Internet, on the telecommunications industry, every bit as much as any U.S. attorney investigating the Mob. The merger of peacetime politics and wartime strategy, the availability of hot, cold, and metaphoric warfare, as well as technologies permitting ongoing surveillance, communication, and easy networking of civilian and military, local and long-distance assets, have made it unrealistic to build a law of war on the fantasy of a demarcated battlefield of uniformed soldiers. For precisely this reason humanitarians have sought to blur the line between human rights and the law in war, and to extend the protections of the classic law in war to guerrilla war, internal conflicts, and all those affected by military violence.

In the summer of 2005, I participated in a lengthy discussion at the Council on Foreign Relations on "postconflict" reconstruction. All agreed we were far from the last century's "world wars." Who was the enemy—and where was the battlefield? The old days of industrial warfare are over—you're not trying to blow stuff up on the battlefield until the political leadership surrenders. It's asymmetric, it's chaotic, its not linear. The battlespace is at once global and intensely local; there are no front lines. Here at home, we hardly seem at war—the enemy, the conflict, the political goal, all have become slippery. At the same time, the modes of "force" have proliferated. Self-defense, war, hostilities, the use of force, resort to arms, police action, peace enforcement, peacemaking, peacekeeping are like "chop," "whip," "blend" on the Cuisinart. Who can align them confidently? They are all technical terms—in military parlance, in legal doctrine, but also in ethical and political discourse.

Military men with experience in Bosnia, Kosovo, Iraq all stressed the continuities of the transition from war to peace—the term "postconflict," they insisted, was a misnomer. In principle, planning and training for the postconflict phase should begin before the conflict, even if it seemed hard to imagine identifying "spare" troops in the preparation phase who might be saved for later tasks. Afterwards, restoring water or eliminating sewage are part of winning the war—postconflict action is the continuation of conflict by other means. Anyway, they wondered, when did the war start—on September 11? In 1991? In 2003?

The boundaries are as blurry on the ground as they are in the rulebook. For the military, everything important and difficult seems to happen in a kind of gray area between war and peace. The idea of a boundary between law enforcement, limited by human rights law, and military action, limited by the laws of armed conflict, seems ever less tenable. In the same city, troops are at once engaging in conflict, stabilizing a neighborhood after conflict, and performing humanitarian, nation-building tasks. Everywhere we find public/private partnerships—outsourcing, insurgents who melt into the mosque, armed soldiers who turn out to work for private contractors. There are civilians all over the battlefield—not only insurgents dressed as refugees, but special forces operatives dressing like natives, private contractors dressing like Arnold Schwarzenegger, and all the civilians running the complex technology and logistical chains "behind" modern warfare.

As a result, the rules of engagement no longer come only from humanitarian law or military discipline—there is also private law, contract, environmental regulation. At one point apparently the Swiss company backing up life insurance contracts for private convoy drivers in Iraq imposed a requirement of additional armed guards if they were to pay on any claim, slowing the whole operation. That's business as usual in the corporate world—but we have long thought war to be different: more violent, and more decisive. Yet the strategies of peace continue in war, and vice versa. We see this when civil affairs officers run after the troops dispensing compensation and apologetic words in a campaign for hearts and minds, or when the military rebuilds what it has destroyed—or the United States finds itself treaty bound to protect the enemies it has remade as the next conflict opens. We know the corporate world can kill—coal miners are killed, truck drivers are killed, a foreseeable number of children die of leukemia downwind from power plants. Law addresses these harms, parsing them out—permissible injuries, or violations of the duty of care. We insure, we contract out, we buy property elsewhere, we zone the city to reduce or concentrate the threat—we sue, we negotiate, we demand regulation or prosecution or the death penalty. Somehow we thought war was different. But it turns out not to be. Violence is one tool among many. And the injuries of wartime are also permissible, privileged, structured by law. In war as in peace, the costs of uncompensated damage are shared and allocated by law.

The modern law of armed conflict reflects efforts by military and humanitarian professionals to respond to these changes in the nature of war, and in our ideas about law itself. Partly this has been a matter of doctrinal ingenuity—adapting doctrinal boundaries of the classic period to keep war special, and to protect the sanctity of the military privilege to kill. Military lawyers and commanders have had to figure out, for example, what weapons you may take, and what rules of engagement apply, if you are heading out of the Green Zone in Baghdad to build a school, or police a neighborhood, or man a checkpoint, or battle insurgents. Should weapons permissible in domestic riot control and policing—nonpenetrating bullets, certain gases—be available? Is this a battlefield? In close quarters on board a ship interdicted during a blockade— should seamen be issued weaponry appropriate for combat or law enforcement? How do we allocate the privilege to kill when combat blurs easily with stabilization and law enforcement?

Updating the law of armed conflict has required more than adapting and applying outmoded rules to new modes of combat. Professionals have also had to learn to deal with a greater degree of uncertainty about what the rules require. The wide use of broad standards, rather than clear rules, encourages— but also requires—a different kind of professional judgment by those on and off the battlefield evaluating the use of force. Commercial actors are quite used to learning that the law is unclear—that the tax management scheme they have come up with might or might not be approved, that their actions might or might not be found to have violated a duty of care. They learn to make strategic use of clear rules and broad standards— "reasonable reliance," "due care," and so forth. They make predictions and take risks in an uncertain legal environment. Sometimes discipline does break down, they skirt too close, are too clever by half. But they can also become savvy players, using legal uncertainty and legal pluralism strategically. Military strategists and humanitarians will need to learn to operate on a similar terrain.

Nevertheless, there remains something troubling about abandoning the world of clear virtue and sharp boundaries for the squishy terrain of the modern law of force. The more profound challenge posed by the modern law of armed conflict arises from the opportunity to rethink the relationship between law and war in more overtly strategic terms. This possibility emerges from several related developments. Ethical and instrumental considerations have been merged in a single legal vocabulary that has been both internalized by the military profession and promoted as a universal vernacular for evaluating the political legitimacy of military action. At the same time, what had been valid distinctions in a law external to military operations—you could look them up in a book and choose to follow or ignore them—have become tools for warfare. Law now offers an institutional and doctrinal space for transforming the boundaries of war into strategic assets, as well as a vernacular for legitimating and denouncing what happens in war. Once the law in war becomes a strategic asset, able to be spoken in multiple voices—an ethically self-confident voice of sharp distinctions, a pragmatic voice of instrumental assessment—we can anticipate that it will be used differently by those with divergent strategic objectives. The resulting legal pluralism itself offers new strategic challenges and opportunities.

As a strategic vernacular, the law in war blends moral and instrumental conversations. The classic law of clear rules and external ethical judgment offered both military and humanitarian professionals a sense of identity and proud self-confidence. Both can be more difficult to come by in the new legal world of more or less. The merger of ethical clarity and instrumental assessment has not always come easily. What, for example, could it *mean* for the distinction between military and civilian to have *itself* become a principle? The "principle of distinction"—there is something oxymoronic here. Either it is a distinction, or it is a principle. What is being demanded: ethical distinction or instrumental calculation? Are you supposed to distinguish—or assess the consequences of distinguishing? How can ethical absolutes and instrumental calculations be made to lie down peacefully together? How can one know what to do, how to judge, whom to denounce? It is not clear, moreover, that we would want the voice of virtue in the war room. Any more than we might want the instrumental voice of military necessity to give expression to our ethics.

The modern law of force offers us two quite different vernaculars for responding to disturbing images from war, such as the Abu Ghraib photos. First—moral outrage. Boundaries have been crossed, for the photos clearly document violations of settled rules. We have repeatedly heard it said that the American administration, like so many others, was "shocked by the photos." Commanders were shocked, senators were shocked, the American public was shocked. Second, we use a vocabulary of more nuanced instrumental calculation: the photos, and the behavior they documented, undermined the war effort. The humiliation of prisoners has no military purpose. Think of the global reaction—thousands of hours building schools, cleaning up garbage, playing soccer with the local kids—all gone in an instant. Both arguments may be right, and both may be effective as persuasion. We can imagine a commander using both to dress down the responsible units. We have heard similar arguments about torture: it is demeaning, unworthy, disgusting—and in any event, not useful. You don't get good information that way.

In one sense, of course, a vocabulary of ethics and instrumental reason is terribly appealing, promising a law about war able to identify opportunities for both moral and pragmatic choice. When we speak about prisoner abuse, it is easy to slide from one rhetoric to the other. Indeed, it is the combination that seems reassuringly watertight—there is simply no argument for this except the perversity of a bad apple. And yet. In a way the recourse to reason also pulls the sting of our shock. Many people may well have been shocked by the photos, but if Secretary of Defense Rumsfeld was shocked, might he not be just a bit too naive to be entrusted with taking the country to war? He was shocked in part, as we all were, because the violence was gratuitous, unnecessary, because it was not instrumentally justified, and, of course, because it was photographed. But was it really not necessary? How does sleep or sensory deprivation compare to humiliation—or to chills, or to intense fear? Which is more humane? Which more effective? Is it correct that torture is *never* effective? Surely it must depend on what kind of torture. Perhaps more severe torture will be more—or less—reliable. But if we are calculating, are we really repulsed? What is the right response? Ensuring respectful treatment for suspected terrorists and insurgents? A prohibition on cameras? Or a careful weighing and balancing of the pain and the gain?

The modern law in war makes it all too easy to shift from one vernacular to another precisely so as to avoid facing the difficult questions opened by either. It also makes it easy to slip into thinking the morally prohibited must have *some* use, something to weigh and balance. At the same time, the voice of outrage distracts us from difficult instrumental questions: Was the problem in Abu Ghraib a legal violation, or a failure of leadership? Insisting that torture is unnecessary brackets questions about the ethics of incarceration, interrogation, or the broader context of postcolonial authority. Was Abu Ghraib a failure of human dignity, or tactics? The whole episode was clearly a military defeat. But we are left with the nagging question. If it could be kept secret, if it could be done pursuant to a warrant, perhaps sexual humiliation can help win the war. It might, on balance, reduce the suffering of civilians and combatants alike. But maybe we just think so because it is off limits, and we're tempted by the common fantasy that the illicit will work.

The slippery slope between moral outrage and instrumental calculation that appears once the law of sharp boundaries begins to break down may be one reason experts have long observed that when warfare itself seems to have no clear beginning or end, no clear battlefield, no clear enemy, military discipline, as well as morale, breaks down. Analysts observed this throughout the twentieth century in postcolonial wars, whether in Algeria or Vietnam or Iraq, in conscript and professional forces alike. Shocking violations of what once seemed clear rules apparently go with the territory—as if it were not all a matter of bad apples and people run amok, but of something new in the making of war. Somehow, a strategic law of tactical distinctions and slippery standards is hard to hold to in combat.

Although it can be troubling to imagine soldiers—or pacifists—thinking strategically about the laws in war, the shift to a strategic legal vernacular has already happened. We simply need to understand it. The fluid modern vocabulary of clear rules and sharp distinctions, broad principles and vague calculations of proportionality and necessity was designed for making distinctions and eroding them, for applying principles and simply invoking them. What we need now is a better understanding of the work of law in military strategy, and of the responsibilities of command in a global political environment structured by this modern law of armed conflict.

As a strategic vocabulary, the law in war blends voices it is hard to imagine harmonizing. There are sharp distinctions and the broad modern standards of proportionality, necessity, and so forth. There are ethical and instrumental considerations. The language is spoken by humanitarian outsiders and military professionals alike, as they defend and denounce the use of force by allies and enemies. The law of armed conflict has become both a professional guide to action and a global political discourse of legitimacy.

The crucial point is that it is not clear which of these many different voices are operative where or when. You cannot go look up your situation in a book and determine whether it is covered by the ethical or the instrumental, the law of sharp or of blurry boundaries, or whether it is to be evaluated by those within or without the military. All these are possible. Each situation might or might not be said to be covered by either. Sometimes it will seem obvious to everyone that this is a case for clear lines, and for ethical validation or denunciation. Sometimes it will not be clear. Whether it is or is not is a function of the consciousness of those who use it. It is in this sense that the law in war has become a "professional" language. It is the ongoing product and expression of a professional milieu. It is used to influence other professionals, and to express one's professional commitments and identity. It is, of course, a very diverse profession—allies and enemies, civilians and soldiers, humanitarians and military planners, statesmen and the media—all participate. In the commercial world, the professional context is also quite diverse: economic competitors, employees, consumers, financiers, and regulators, across a global market, may all speak the same legal language. Using law strategically means identifying openings that can be made to seem persuasive, or anticipating reactions that will invalidate what may have seemed clear to you.

In war, many strategic decisions have a similar structure: Is this a case for clarity about what is and is not permissible, or for a gradation of more and less? Humanitarian and military professionals need to decide whether it seems advantageous to insist upon a sharp distinction or a soft continuum between war and peace, combat and humanitarian relief, conventional and unconventional weapons, and so forth. Is this a situation for clear boundaries and on/off judgments, or should we treat it as a matter of more or less? Should we pull back to the classic distinctions of war and peace, civilian and combatant, or embrace the modern law of proportionality? Would we benefit from a firewall between these two situations, or not? These decisions will need to be made in relationship to an audience, and will require an attitude about the appropriate tolerated residual violation of—and opposition to—whatever approach we adopt.

Take the difficult question of when war ends. The answer is not to be found in law or fact, but in strategy. Declaring the end of hostilities might be a matter of election theater or military assessment, just like announcing that there remains "a long way to go," or that the "insurgency is in its final throes." Declaring war, declaring not-war, or not-declaring-war all need to be seen—alongside the actual use of force—as instruments of warfare. To recognize this is not to abandon the old distinctions—we may often want to insist upon a bright line. For the military, defining the battlefield may still define the privilege to kill.[4] And humanitarians also sometimes want to define the not-battlefield to open a space for humanitarian action. Aid agencies want the guys digging the wells to be seen as humanitarians, not postconflict combatants. Distinguishing—alongside balancing—has become at once a mode of warfare and of pacifism.

Ending conflict, calling it occupation, ending occupation, calling it sovereignty—then opening hostilities, calling it a police action, suspending the judicial requirements of policing, declaring a state of emergence, a zone of insurgency—all these things are also tactics in the conflict. We are occupying, but Fallujah, for a few weeks, is again a combat zone, and so on. This is a war, this is an occupation, this is a police action, this is a security zone. These are insurgents, those are criminals, these are illegal combatants, and so on. All these assertions take the form of factual or legal assessments, but we should also understand them as arguments, at once messages and weapons. Communicating the war is fighting the war, and law—legal categorization—is a communication tool. Defining the battlefield is not only a matter of deployed force, or privileging killing; it is also a rhetorical claim.

Moreover, the normative framework within which claims of this type can be made has expanded. The claim is not made only in the vernacular of the law in war—it is also a claim in the fields of American constitutional law and foreign affairs law, as well as federal courts, administrative, criminal, and military law. And in the international law of human rights. In today's wars, police and combat operations run side by side, and the zone of combat abuts and overlaps the zones of occupation and military action. The war stretches simultaneously across Missouri and Cuba and Poland and Iraq. Dozens of legal regimes operate concurrently across the battlespace. Saying human rights norms apply to combat is an assertion—like saying humanitarian actors on the battlefield need to abide by humanitarian law. The assertion that human rights limits action in combat will seem persuasive to some audiences in some situations, as will the assertion that the activities are distinct, the laws separate.

In war, as in peace, strategic claims are made to audiences. The president declares the war ongoing. For the detainees at Guantanamo the "war" may never end. What war, which war—the war on terror? The war on poverty? On Al Qaeda? On Iraq? The Taliban? Afghanistan? The war for security, for oil, for . . . The object that, once achieved, will end their war remains vague. The Bush administration's ability to extend the war for which they are held indefinitely is not limited by a legal norm, standing out there someplace yelling at him to stop. It is limited by the power of those who find his claim of continuing authority, continuing necessity, unpersuasive to convince the administration to change course. That could be American courts, legislators, media personalities, Republican Party funders, allied nations, the German chancellor, or people in other countries whose outrage about Guantanamo can be translated into increasing the costs for the administration to pursue its objectives.

The development of a more flexible law in war has complex effects for the military professional seeking to defend the use of force on the battlefield. Military leaders will want to condition the battlespace by informing relevant publics, including their own troops, that civilians will be killed, that these killings are privileged by the law in war, and that these deaths are permissible collateral damage. The identification of prohibited acts—and the attention paid to investigating and assessing their proportionality—will leave a great deal of the battlespace open for action, before and afterwards. An attack will not only be judged ex post, it will also be judged beforehand by expectations, and during execution by all those who participate or witness it. The form and timing of the assessment are also, in part, open to strategy—when should what be disclosed?

The law in war places a burden of justification on those who assault undefended civilians, cultural monuments, churches, or medical facilities, but assaults on these targets are permissible in some circumstance—if necessary and proportional to a legitimate military objective, including self-defense. Debating an attack in these terms focuses our attention on the circumstances. Military professionals typically do this from the perspective of the soldier who acted. Given what he or she knew, was the attack proportional and legitimate? The circumstances will mean, in large part, what the enemy did, or was expected to do, or had a habit of doing. Perfidious attacks by insurgents dressed as civilians, antiaircraft weaponry mounted on hospitals or religious institutions will ratchet up the legitimacy of the attack. And of course, other audiences will look at it differently: given how powerful America is, did they need to kill my husband?

Moreover, people will identify the military purpose in different ways. Could we imagine an attack on a church whose *military purpose* was to focus public attention on the enemy's perfidy? Or, perhaps more plausibly, whose purpose was to distract public attention from another attack elsewhere? Might a commander disclose the abuse of prisoners, distribute photos, not only to control the timing and context for their discovery, but also to draw the media, and the opposition, and the enemy to their evaluation? Could we imagine abusing prisoners in the first place precisely for this purpose? Perhaps we could not. But others will have no trouble imagining these things. And if they do, how will they imagine the proportionality of the strike?

Suddenly, the prosecution of a military campaign looks a lot like a political campaign. The impact of law in war debates about specific incidents on the broader military campaign will be difficult to assess in advance. Focus on the dead children in the church foyer, whether or not their death turns out to have been permissible collateral damage, may inoculate the public against those who might oppose the war more broadly. The prisoner abuse scandal—like the rights of the Guantanamo detainees—may have functioned in this way, as an outlet for criticism that might otherwise have been directed at the broader war. But the reverse can certainly also happen, even if legitimate, harsh treatment of prisoners or dead civilians may fire up the opposition to the broader effort. These effects may be different for different audiences. We can imagine the American Democratic party glad to have the Guantanamo prisoners to focus on, and federal courts to do the work of judgment, rather than being forced to assess the broader war. But we can imagine Palestinian refugees watching television moved by the death of Iraqi civilians regardless of how we interpret the legal defensibility of their demise.

Lawfare—managing law and war together—requires a strategic assessment of these various claims, and active strategy by military and humanitarian actors to frame the situation to their advantage. Military and humanitarian professionals make strategic assessments about the solidity of the boundary between war and peace all the time, insisting on the absolute privilege to kill or the inviolability of those outside combat when it seems more advantageous than an assessment of proportionality and vice versa. In these strategic assessments, the legal questions becomes these: Who, understanding the law in what way, will be able to do what to affect our ongoing efforts? How, using what mix of behavior and assertion, can we transform the strategic situation to our advantage?

We might see this as public relations—shaping expectations

about what will happen and what will be legitimate. But this is more than using legal language in the media to describe and defend what you will do anyway for other military purposes. This also means doing things as a message—as an assertion of right, an expression of intent and resolve, or to alter the landscape on which the legitimacy of your campaign will be judged.

We have left the world of legal validity behind, except as a claim made to an audience. But we have also left the world of persuasion behind, except as a rather superficial description of what we mean by using force—or language—strategically. The audiences for our action are not inert judges, waiting to be persuaded. They are also participants, with their own strategies. They hear what we say—or see what we do—and they interpret it as a strategy. As something we said or did for effect. And, of course, their reaction will also be strategic, and we will interpret it strategically. Our allies may say they are persuaded, our enemies that they are not. The vernacular shapes those responses by making some claims seem more or less plausible, more or less something one would only say mendaciously. In this environment, the impact of our actions and claims will depend upon on more than the validity or persuasiveness of our claims. We will need a complex social analysis of the dynamic interaction between ideas about the law and strategic objectives.

Thinking about law strategically sharpens awareness of these multiple perspectives. Yet many discussions of the law in war—and of disarmament more generally—continue to assume that both sides in a military conflict will share an interest in the law in war. All military professionals share an interest, it is said, in the elimination of unnecessary suffering on—and off—the battlefield. When stated in such general terms, this may also seem to apply to humanitarian professionals. And for that matter, to civilians—indeed it may seem to be in the universal interest of all mankind. Everyone benefits when there is a clear firebreak between conventional and unconventional weapons, or when there is a mutually accepted sense for the privileged and the perfidious in battle. But once we recognize the law in war as a strategic tool, this confidence seems misplaced.

Where it is clear, the law in war will have winners and losers. Battling in the shadow of the law, some will find their strength multiplied, others will find their available tactics stigmatized. It is unlikely both sides in a conflict, given the contextual differences between their military, political, and economic assets, will evaluate the desirability of various laws of armed conflict similarly. Weapons of mass destruction—or perfidious acts of other sorts—are unlikely to be seen as equally "special" on both sides of a conflict.

At the same time, where the law is open and plural, it will be pulled and pushed in different directions, articulated in conflicting ways, by those with different strategic objectives. Where it is to our advantage to insist on clear rules and sharp distinctions, our adversaries might well benefit from a law that calculated proportionality, and vice versa. We will need to learn to operate in a complex world of legal pluralism, of multiple perspectives on the validity, persuasiveness, and strategic usefulness of legal norms and institutional competence.

Opposing sides in war will seldom choose the same time and place for battle, for strategy is all about determining when and where so as to benefit one's own force. The same is true for the law in war. Where firm rules distinguishing war and peace—or a firebreak between types of weapons—will benefit one side, they will by definition not benefit the other. This is certainly the case in today's asymmetric wars between forces with radically different technological, financial, and political resources. When the United States conditions the battlefield by asserting its privilege to kill, we can expect its enemies, whatever their own tactics, to insist that every dead civilian evidences callous disregard for the law in war. And we can expect both claims to be believed by some relevant audiences.

It is unlikely, moreover, that those seeking to legitimate and delegitimate a given use of force will choose the same rhetorical weapon. As the military assures us the dead civilians were unavoidable collateral damage, humanitarians will insist that the death of every civilian is an outrageous violation. Where the military insists on the privilege to kill, the humanitarian will call the killing unnecessary, disproportional in a campaign that is itself unjust and illegitimate. Military and humanitarian professionals will rarely evaluate the strategic usefulness of sharp and fuzzy distinctions in a given case the same way. Where the military may want to blur combat, occupation, and school building, the humanitarian agencies may want to clarify that building this school is not part of the war machine.

This strategic terrain becomes blurrier still when we begin to merge economic and civilian administration into military operations, or when occupation and ongoing battle take place side by side. When the occupying force manages the water supply, the electrical grid, the medical system, or divides the pathways of commercial life with checkpoints, or implements a new national development strategy, the occupying power will have set up pressure points it will be difficult not to instrumentalize for political—or military—purposes. Should there be a firewall between the civilian and military administration, between the State Department and the Pentagon, between the American and Iraqi security forces or civilian administrations? Should we *say* there is a firewall—should we do what can be done to send the message that there is a firewall? How much can we use the checkpoints—or the cement contracts—to pressure and reward supporters in the broader conflict? And why not shut the city to commerce to flush out the insurgents—why not use economic and legal levers to consolidate the authority of those least likely to resist the occupation? If we can imagine doing it, they can imagine our doing it. Our efforts to distinguish our violence from our civilian administration may well run into their claims of illegitimate purpose and disproportionate cost.

The point here is not that the modern law in war permits one to say anything, although in the cacophony of interpretation that follows a military strike it can often seem that way. The point is that the split deep within the law in war between a voice of ethics and consequences, a voice of boundaries and gradations, a voice of rules and of standards, gives rise to a particular kind of conversation when it is deployed by people inside and outside the military, or on opposite sides of a military conflict. It is a conversation focused on questions of distinction—firebreak or continuum?—in which it is easy to over- or underestimate the stability and persuasiveness of arguments either way, and in which players on opposing sides are playing the same cards in different ways.

Sometimes, of course, parties on both sides of a conflict can see things similarly—or can communicate strategically by settings and respecting sharp boundaries, or by evaluating the legitimacy of military action by one or the other side in similar ways. A formal boundary between conventional and unconventional weaponry might seem to those on various possible sides of a conflict desirable to channel and caution the decisionmaker and to facilitate clear communication between estranged parties: here you are crossing a very significant line. Many analysts remain convinced the United States and China carried on a subtle and implicit dialogue about the limits of their commitment to Vietnam begun by the U.S. failure to take out the dikes and dams to flood northern cities. Military and humanitarian professionals have joined forces to build a regime for chemical weapons on precisely this idea, formalizing a firebreak between chemical and other weaponry. We prevent soldiers from using tear gas, permissible in our public square, to clear the cave in combat because we fear we will be licensing the enemy to ratchet things up, across the boundary, to gas.

Then again, once we are at war, it can seem—to military or humanitarian professionals—neither ethically nor strategically wise to respect these artificial boundaries. We need to remember that what seemed solid can indeed melt into air. Indeed, sometimes we can make that happen ourselves. And when that happens, the boundary can come to seem unpersuasive. Take the clear and sensible firebreak between chemical and other weapons. Now we need to clear a cave. If we use tear gas, will the enemy say—will they be believed—that we have used a weapon of mass destruction? But perhaps no one brought tear gas along, in case we got captured and someone could say we were equipped to use gas on the battlefield. So we use an incendiary device instead. Will they say—will they be believed—that we have used wildly disproportionate force to achieve our objective? Under pressure, confidence in the firebreak can be eroded. The humanism of effects-based targeting, the perceived legitimacy of the broader conflict in the eyes of politically relevant audiences, can trump the clarity of the prohibition. These are the thoughts that transform ethical considerations into multilevel game theory. And yes, something has been lost.

Or, to take another example, it can seem urgent—morally and strategically—to ensure that there be a firebreak between conventional and nuclear war. After all, with nuclear weapons we are talking about blowing up the world. Or are we? The doctrine of mutual assured destruction (MAD), built to guarantee the firebreak by threatening to respond to any first use with overwhelming force, never sounded either ethically defensible or credible. In ethical terms, the acronym said it all. But also in strategic terms, more flexible uses, tactical uses, seemed attractive. Many scholars who modeled the implicit negotiations between the estranged blocs in the Cold War concluded that a sharp distinction between nuclear and nonnuclear battle would help stabilize the situation as one of coexistence. But there were always other voices, urging the United States to develop more flexible options, or more effective missile defenses, that might upset the balance. Often these calculations relied on assessments of the broader context: a conflict between open democracies and closed totalitarian societies, between economically robust and economically stagnant powers, and so forth. In these circumstances, they argued, destabilizing the equilibrium would create a positive spiral in our direction—spending them into defeat, while relying on the deterrent effect of appearing just crazy enough ourselves to cross the firebreak at the least provocation.

Once you start picking away at this notion, it becomes plausible that nuclear weapons might not be the problem, but might sometimes be part of the solution, as a matter of instrumental and moral calculus. Take Hiroshima: perhaps the real problem was the allied war aim of "unconditional surrender." What if you are a small nation, facing the enmity of the world, and of the world's greatest military power. Wouldn't nuclear weapons be the most efficient, the most humane, national strategy? And maybe it is right that all the dangers are at the start in the first round of nuclear proliferation. Once the arms race gets underway, a kind of stability sets in. How terrible are nuclear weapons—what should we weigh them against, anyway? Firebombing? Or precision strikes, or suicide attacks?

Something is undeniably lost when an ethically self-confident law is transformed into a strategic discourse. If things go well, professionals become more sensitive to the multiple perspectives that go with legal pluralism. But they also come to evaluate war from the viewpoint of war. The strategic calculations of warfare have become the only limit on warfare, as they have merged with the vernacular of political life. This is quite different from saying the political interests of states continue to trump the law. Neorealism of that type is simply out of touch with the vernacular of modern politics and the practice of modern warfare. But there is little comfort in knowing that law has become the vernacular for evaluating the legitimacy of war and politics where it has done so by itself becoming a strategic instrument of war and the continuation of politics by similar means.

Soldiers have always found it disorienting—if also sometimes exhilarating—to cross the line from civilian life to the battlefield and back again. While in war, there is danger and freedom. In battle, soldiers have always slipped the collar of chickenshit regulations. They have also often violated clear and significant rules. Afterward they could be reassured—or disciplined. Increasingly, they are called upon to exercise the judgments of civilian life in war. The difficulty is no longer to make the transition from peace to war and back—but to metabolize their astonishing proximity and juxtaposition. It is not surprising that soldiers would find their judgments about the applicability of standards like "self-defense" or "necessity" becoming unmoored, in part because of the rapidly shifting perspectives, from near and far, that can be brought to bear on their action.

Terms like "proportional" or "necessary" are stabilized by shared cultural assumptions that can be quite local or specific to a profession. Military pilots—and infantry—learn from their colleagues, as well as from the rules of engagement, how trigger-happy they can be in "self-defense." Or how aggressive they can be when interrogating a detainee. As any anthropologist will report, it can be terribly difficult to sort out the origin, range, and mode of reproduction for such loose cultural norms. Why did it seem plausible to photograph people being humiliated or threatened by dogs? Was it a few impressionable young soldiers under the influence of a one sadist? Or was it the general atmosphere created in Washington by the president and secretary of defense that the war on terror justified extraordinary means at all levels? It may well have been both—and many things in between.

In any event, once the local culture got going at Abu Ghraib, it held pretty well—until the perspective shifted. Until someone else got wind of it, or photos got out, and it was broadcast around the world. Suddenly local—even intensely private or personal—judgments are rejudged by many others from wildly different perspectives. When this happens, the local moral and professional fabric is torqued sharply. Only the most experienced politicians or military commanders could be expected to keep their footing when the ground shifts so radically.

In today's asymmetric postcolonial wars, the terrain beneath a soldier's interpretations of what is and is not appropriate is constantly shifting. The tendency simultaneously to dehumanize and to identify with enemy soldiers goes with the

experience of warfare. Traditionally, the law in war helps stabilize the situation—you are permitted to kill here, these people,
this way. American soldiers in Iraq express both contempt for
and comprehension of the perfidious tactics of their adversaries. The Iraqi "only understands force," and fights in ways
that violate every rule in the book: dressing like a civilian, hid-
ing in mosques, sending women as suicide bombers. At the
same time, the sympathy expressed by many American soldiers
for their Iraqi adversaries is striking. Many say things like,
"How would I feel if this were my hometown?" And against a
foe so technologically superior, able to remove himself almost
completely from the battlefield, how else could one fight? The
modern law of armed conflict brings clarity when it marks the
American effort as legitimate, the American tactics as humane,
the Iraqi response perfidious.

But the insurgents have a point of view, which can also be
expressed in the vocabulary of the modern law. And their
claims also sometimes persuade. The Americans also seem to
be crossing boundaries, using force that can seem to those on
the other side to be disproportionate and illegitimate.

That soldiers are changed by war, and disoriented by the
move from civilian life to the battlefield and back, is a staple of
war literature. As the boundaries around the battlefield soften,
and the media makes every local judgment potentially available for simultaneous reevaluation in living rooms everywhere,
the anxiety that accompanies the juxtaposition of one's own
perspective at war and in peace is concentrated in the mind of
every soldier. The many memoirs that have emerged from
America's recent wars are filled with the difficulty of relating
war and peace in real time. Soldiers and pilots and commanders must reckon with the knowledge that their local battlefield
culture—and the privilege to kill—is unstable and subject to

reevaluation, by their enemies, by their commanders, by their families, and by themselves.

The problem is not simply awareness that other people speak the same law differently, or have different perspectives on the legitimate and the illegitimate. It is also increasingly clear to all those who use the modern law in war that claims made in its name are indeed made strategically. They are things people say for a reason, to get a reaction—as a tactic, as propaganda. As a result, we are increasingly likely to interpret *whatever* military or humanitarian professionals say about the use of force in strategic terms—as something they said for tactical advantage. As professionals—civilian or military—we know how to make and unmake the distinctions between war and peace, civilian and combatant. And we know they do too.

This can have an odd effect: as we use the discourse more, we believe it less—at least when spoken by others. *Their* arguments are as prone to mendacity as their tactics to perfidy. Our own arguments, by contrast, seem overwhelmingly persuasive—what else could we have done? When this dynamic gets going, the vernacular that promised a common conversation has produced a dialogue of the deaf. But of course, the opposing speakers are not the only audience—and it will be easy for both to lose track of the natural human reaction of those outside the field of combat to experience themselves as difference splitters, and to be blindsided when our allies do not find our defenses airtight. But then again, perhaps we do realize this. Wouldn't the sensible thing be to heighten our claims, push the extreme, and draw the difference-splitters toward us? Perhaps—although we know this can backfire, and they can flip to the other side. Nevertheless, the strategic considerations bearing on our approach have multiplied wildly.

When the law of armed combat is used as a strategic vocabulary of legitimacy, in this sense, it can undermine itself. As people embrace the law in war strategically, they may lose confidence in its plausibility as a mark of legitimacy. This could be avoided if we imagined a sharp distinction between professionals, who used the language instrumentally or strategically, and a lay public, who consumed it as a mark of legitimacy or virtue. The difficulty, however, is that professionals also want to experience the vocabulary as a mark of ethics and legitimacy. The audience for our professional claims is, increasingly, also composed of people—whether professional or lay—who are adept at mobilizing the language of the law for instrumental or strategic ends.

We have a new vocabulary, a new terrain of strategic thought, a new way to communicate our intentions and legitimate our action. Put in operation, the new law in war can also be profoundly unsettling. You may remember U.S. Major General James Mattis, poised to invade Fallujah, concluding his demand that the insurgents stand down with these words: "We will always be humanitarian in all our efforts. We will fight the enemy on our terms. May God help them when we're done with them."[5] The juxtaposition of humanitarian claims and blunt threats is jarring. But we should try to analyze his remark strategically. In what ways did this statement—this interpretation of the relationship between the laws in war and the battle to come—work to condition the battlefield?

Mattis was affirming that he would follow the law of armed conflict to the letter, might even exceed it, would certainly embody its humanitarian spirit—but that he would prevail. We will need to understand how this sounds, particularly in asymmetric war, when the law of armed conflict has so often been a vocabulary used by the rich to judge the poor. When the Iraqi insurgent quoted on the same page of the *New York Times* as

Mattis threatened to decapitate civilian hostages if the coalition forces did not withdraw, he was also threatening innocent civilian death—less of it actually—but without the humanitarian promise.

We need to understand the effects of saying, as you stand poised to invade a town, that you will be "humanitarian" in all you do. Those effects will depend on how the statements were received, in the first place, by people with the capacity to influence the military operations. Major General Mattis's remarks made me shiver—but never mind that. I am far from the action.

Coalition troops might have heard him. Their families at home might have read his remarks. We need to sort out their reactions, and understand how the commitment to "be humanitarian" might influence who was willing to do what to further the cause. Perhaps Mattis was also speaking, at least in part, to the insurgents. Telling them to stand down. He might have been saying, "We'll play by the rules, and we expect you to do so as well," although this seems a rather ham-handed way to communicate such a message. Maybe a more likely message is something like, "Don't think just because we follow the rules we won't be tough—nor will your own perfidy defeat us." Perhaps—but how did he sound to settlers in Gaza, to civilians in Pakistan, or Holland, or the UK? And how would their impressions in turn condition Mattis's battlefield?

I doubt the insurgents were speaking to Mattis when they threatened to decapitate their hostages, although they may have been. There is no question the insurgents' treats—and practices—of perfidy changed the terrain on which they operate, intimidating civilians and humanitarian workers, changing the standard operating procedures for the occupying authorities. They also communicated something of their resolve—and their otherness—to the technologically superior military professionals against whom they struggled. We should imagine that they, like Mattis, were speaking about the law in war strategically—to persuade. They were speaking to a public, a world public, whose reaction they hoped would strengthen their strategic hand. They may, of course, have hardened Mattis's resolve, American resolve, the revulsion of the global citizenry. When the poor deviate from the best military practices of the rich, it is tempting to treat their entire campaign as illegitimate. But before we jump to the legitimacy of their cause, how should we evaluate the strategic use of perfidy by every outgunned insurgency battling a modern occupation army?

At the same time, it is no secret that technological advances have heightened the asymmetry of warfare, or that the insurgents find themselves massively outgunned by coalition forces who have removed themselves almost entirely from the battleground. The vulnerability of the occupation forces to suicide bombing and improvised explosive devices has been well reported, alongside the difficulty of gaining operational intelligence about who and where the insurgents are where the citizenry broadly sympathizes with their cause, or has been intimidated by their acts. But we must also remember the relative invulnerability of coalition forces to anything *except* suicide bombs, the difficulty of getting near enough without dressing as a civilian, the impossibility of gaining a view of the battlespace without climbing a minaret. In that context, a law of armed conflict that renders the American assault on Fallujah "humanitarian" and the insurgent response "perfidy" will not be equally persuasive for all audiences. Those who sympathize with the insurgents will either treat the law in war as the ally and tool of their adversary—or they will reinterpret its terms more favorably to their own cause. Probably some of both.

From an effects-based perspective, perfidious attacks on our military—from mosques, by insurgents dressing as civilians or using human shields—may have more humanitarian consequences than any number of alternative tactics. And, more importantly, they are very likely to be interpreted by many as reasonable, "fair" responses by a massively outgunned, but legitimate force. There is no question that technological asymmetry erodes the persuasiveness of the "all bound by the same rules" idea. It should not be surprising that forces with vastly superior arms and intelligence capacity are held to a higher standard in the court of world public opinion than their adversaries. As persuasion, the law in force has indeed become a sliding scale.

Working strategically with such a law in war will be a far more complex matter than insisting that we followed all the universally valid rules. In 1996, I traveled to Senegal as a civilian instructor with the Naval Justice School out of Newport to train members of the Senegalese military in the laws of war and human rights. At the time, the training program was operating in fifty-three countries, from Albania to Zimbabwe. As I recall it, our training message was clear: humanitarian law is not a way of being nice. By internalizing human rights and humanitarian law, you will make your force interoperable with international coalitions, suitable for international peacekeeping missions. To use our sophisticated weapons, your military culture must have rules of operation and engagement parallel to our own.

Most importantly, we insisted, humanitarian law will make your military more effective—will make your use of force something you can sustain and proudly stand behind. When we broke into small groups for simulated exercises, a regional commander kept asking the hard questions. When you capture some guerrillas, isn't it better to place a guy's head on a stake for deterrence? Well, no, we would patiently explain, this will strengthen the hostility of villagers to your troops, and imagine what would happen if CNN were nearby. They would all laugh—of course, we must be sure the press stays away.

Ah, but this is no longer possible, we said—if you want to play on the international stage, you need to be ready to have CNN constantly by your side. You must place an imaginary CNN webcam on your helmet, or, better, just over your shoulder. Not because force must be limited and not because CNN might show up—but because only force that can imagine itself to be seen can be enduring. An act of violence one can disclose and be proud of is ultimately stronger, more *legitimate*.

Indeed, we might imagine calculating a CNN effect, in which the additional opprobrium resulting from civilian deaths, discounted by the probability of their becoming known to relevant audiences, multiplied by the ability of that audience to hinder the continued prosecution of the war, will need to be added to the probable costs of the strike in calculating its proportionality and necessity—as well as its tactical value and strategic consequences. Our lesson in Senegal was written completely in the key of persuasion—not validity. The point was to understand the rules that would be understood by others to apply—and to conduct operations in ways that would be understood by others to be legitimate. The law of armed conflict provide a lexicon for figuring out what will be understood to apply and be legitimate—but only if we think of those rules through the eyes of those we would like to validate our action. This was a lesson apparently lost on those who considered the interrogation of "high-value targets" in our own war on terror. Nevertheless, the Senegalese had learned—as Secretary Rumsfeld now seems to be learning—what was required for a culture of violence to be something one could proudly stand behind. What was required, in a word, for warfare to be civilized.

Legal War and the Elusive Experience of Responsibility

It is cold comfort to think that two hundred years of effort by humanitarian and military professionals has brought forth a law that marks warfare as a civilized activity. But there is a further difficulty. The transformation of the law in war into a vocabulary of persuasion about legitimacy can erode the sense of professional and ethical responsibility for our decisions—as humanitarians or military professionals. We no longer need to decide for ourselves whether war is civilized, whether killing this civilian is a good idea, whether attacking the town is ethically defensible. The law of armed conflict will do that for us—while lending itself to our strategic deployment.

It is easy to see in retrospect that something is lost when we begin to parse the decision to bomb Hiroshima and Nagasaki in these terms. We start with the legitimacy of the conflict, we accept the political decision to insist upon unconditional surrender, we then evaluate, from the position of the American command, knowing what they knew then, whether the attack was necessary and proportional to the military objective. We come quickly to weighing and balancing—the horrifying death of so many, against the costs of an invasion. We begin to make comparisons—the firebombing of Tokyo, also horrifying, but less effective in crumbling Japanese will, and so on. Yet more seems lost when we treat these comparisons and calculations as strategic elements in the conflict itself. Over time, we have repeatedly announced that in Hiroshima and Nagasaki we were, in fact, humanitarian in all that we did. The calculation satisfied the American public immediately, and has held ever since. And historians have long suggested that whether intended or not, the idea that nuclear first use was acceptable to the American command and public sent a message to the Soviet Union.

The idea that a nuclear strike might be a civilized, humanitarian act in war can seem shocking. But even the World Court has held that the laws governing nuclear weapons are no different from those governing other weapons—their use must respect the principles of distinction, proportionality, necessity. Of course there were those who argued to the court that nuclear weapons, by their very nature, *could not* respect these principles—but there also were those, including representatives of the nuclear powers, who said their use might sometimes be justified. In conversations about proliferation, the positions can be reversed: the nuclear powers insisting on the firebreak; vulnerable pariah states seeing the acquisition of nuclear weapons as a reasonable and legitimate strategy of self-defense.

We should not be shocked that states living in one or another way under the security of the nuclear umbrella—the nuclear powers and their allies—would see nuclear proliferation differently from states who feel threatened by the nuclear powers. Or that both would find ways to express their viewpoints—both would, in fact, be able to find their viewpoints, in the shared legal and political vernacular of sovereign prerogative and international responsibility. It might, of course, be that the law is simply the clear tool of the nuclear states, but it is more likely if we think about it, and listen as people argue about it, that we will find it open-ended enough to nurture the legitimate interests of all states, and to both legitimate and delegitimate the use and acquisition of nuclear weapons. As both sides use this vernacular, they will root their sense of entitlement in the situation as they see it. When we listen to Vitoria now, it seems outrageous that he should have found in the Indian's common humanity a justification for their slaughter by the Spanish should they not yield to Christian proselytizing. In our own time, our professional vocabularies blunt the sense of shock when the acquisition and use of nuclear weapons has everyone claiming only to respond, and no one feeling responsible.

When we encourage the military to have lawyers pore over the targets to be struck in Iraq, or to instruct their troops in the law of armed conflict, we are not only encouraging a particular language of evaluation. We are also allowing that language to substitute for other judgments. The legal language has become capacious enough to give the impression that by using it, one will have "taken everything into account" or "balanced" all the relevant competing considerations. This is the basis for the claim that adding lawyers to the mix can improve one's strategic analysis.

But it is extremely difficult to see how one might, in fact, weigh and balance civilian deaths against military objectives. The idea of proportionality—or necessity—encourages a kind of strategy, and ethic, by metaphor: the metaphor of weighing and balancing. I have learned that if you ask a military professional precisely how many civilians you *can* kill to offset how much risk to one of your own men, you won't receive a straight answer. When the Senegalese asked us, we'd say, "It's a judgment call." Indeed, at least so far as I have been able to ascertain, there is no background exchange rate for civilian life. What you find instead are rules kicking the decision up the chain of command as the number of civilians increases, until the decision moves offstage from military professionals to politicians. Rules transforming weighing and balancing effects into attributions of responsibility.

In the early days of the Iraq war, coalition forces were certainly frustrated by Iraqi soldiers who advanced in the company of civilians. A Corporal Mikael McIntosh reported that he and a colleague had declined several times to shoot soldiers in fear of harming civilians. "It's a judgment call." he said, "if the risks outweigh the losses, then you don't take the shot." He offered an example: "There was one Iraqi soldier, and 25 women and children, I didn't take the shot." His colleague, Sergeant Eric Schrumpf chipped in to describe facing one soldier among two or three civilians, opening fire, and killing civilians: "We dropped a few civilians, but what do you do. I'm sorry, but the chick was in the way."[6]

There is no avoiding decisions of this type in warfare. The difficulty arises when humanitarian law transforms *decisions* about whom to kill into *judgments*, when it encourages us to think the chick's death resulted not from an exercise of human freedom, for which a moral being is responsible, but rather from the abstract operation of professional principles. We know there are clear cases both ways—destroying the village to save it, or minor accidental damage en route to victory—but we also know that the principles are *most* significant in the great run of situations that fall in between. What does it mean to pretend these decisions are principled judgments? How should we evaluate the irreducibly imaginary quality of the promise that costs and benefits will be weighed, that warfare will be proportional, its violence necessary?

There is no question that metaphoric weighing and balancing will be done differently in different quarters. A great deal will depend on the ambit of one's sense of professional responsibility. In the Gulf War, who should have weighed the postwar civilian deaths from cholera against the allied decision to take out the generator hulls? Should the pilot told to take out the generators have balanced this or that approach route, hitting this or that component of the generator, against the postwar effects on the water supply given the cost of repairs under different attack plans—or just the likelihood of hitting the church next door or of killing civilian maintenance men inside at different times of day? What about when the military leadership decides to take out the electricity to degrade the enemy's communication network and capacity to coordinate batteries of surface-to-air missiles? In such a calculation there will always be something to put on the other side—some military objective or other, unless the violence is truly wanton. What about the political leadership deciding to launch the campaign in the first place? What if they didn't know how long it would take to get the generators back up and running? What if they didn't know how long the war would last?

Parceling out responsibility and ensuring that everyone evaluates the proportionality of what they do can also ensure that no one notices the likely deaths from cholera. And, if no one noticed, and it was no one's job to notice, then perhaps no one was responsible, no one did decide—they just died. Or maybe it was all Saddam Hussein's fault, after all—he started the war, and afterwards, he could have sped repairs of the electricity grid rather than his own grid of palaces and security. But then, we remember Iran's claim before the World Court that the conflict with the United States had begun long before—in the 1950s—and that the taking of American diplomatic hostages would need to be evaluated in the "proper context, namely the whole political dossier of the relations between

Iran and the United States of America over the last 25 years."[7] Or the American assertion before the World Court that one should assess the mining of Nicaragua's harbor in the full context of ongoing peace negotiations and the history of Nicaragua's efforts to destabilize the neighborhood.[8]

Evaluated ex post, things will look different, of course. A great deal will depend on how the war itself is remembered—and who won. We can expect revision of the story itself to become a tactic. Looking back on Hiroshima, it has become routine in the United States to assume that an invasion of the Japanese homeland was the necessary counter to be placed at the other end of the scale when weighing and balancing the decision to drop the bomb. Putting ourselves back in the legitimate position of the Truman's wartime decision-making, we ask: how many allied soldiers were saved by the bomb? Not Japanese civilians or soldiers but Allied soldiers against Japanese bomb deaths. Estimates differ. In June 1945, the Joint Chiefs estimated 40,000. In 1945, Truman said he had estimated 250,000. In his memoirs, written ten years after the fact, Truman used the figure 500,000. Churchill, in 1953, estimated a million Americans and 500,000 British troops. In 1991, President Bush claimed the use of atomic bombs had "spared millions of American lives."[9]

One thing that is going on here is a loss in the experience of responsibility—command responsibility, ethical responsibility, political responsibility—as the scale tilts overwhelmingly toward the mercy of bombing. I was struck that Iraq war reporting was filled with anecdotes about soldiers overcome by remorse at having slaughtered civilians—and being counseled back to duty by their officers, their chaplains, their mental health professionals, who explained that what they had done was necessary, proportional, and therefore just. Of course, if you ask leading humanitarian law experts how many civilians you can kill for this or that, you will also not get an answer. Rather than saying, "It's a judgment call," however, they are likely to say something like, "You just can't target civilians"— thereby refusing to engage in the pragmatic assessments necessary to make that rule applicable in combat, defaulting, if you will, to the external strategy of denunciation abandoned a century ago by humanitarian law.

In psychological terms, it is hard to avoid interpreting this pragmatism-promised-but-not-delivered as a form of denial, a collaborative denial—by humanitarians and military lawyers— of their participation in the machinery of war. In the military vernacular, it might be more accurate to sense a collaborative avoidance of responsibility, of command responsibility and leadership—that is, eagerness to push responsibility up to the domain of politics or down to the domain of rules. In this sense, the modern law in war is less the shrewd stuff of strategy than it is a delusional escape from responsibility.

The law in warfare is not only about what is legitimate or civilized behavior in wartime—it is also, more overtly, about responsibility. The law of force divides political responsibility for the decision to go to war (and the law of war) from military responsibility for action on the battlefield (the law in war). Unbundling the exercise of sovereignty and rethinking war as a range of related public acts on a continuum from more to less violent, more to less differentiated from the governmental routines of peacetime or the ongoing pressures and coercions of international commerce life, increases the range of options for military and political leaders alike. Of course statesmen have always threatened and cajoled as well as attacked, but we now have a well-organized gradation of threats and sanctions and boycotts whose scale is widely understood by allies and potential enemies alike, and whose deployment can be shared out among a range of institutional actors, both multilateral and unilateral.

Not all threats, not all sanctions, not all rewards, need come from the unified command. There is the United Nations. But there are also American corporate actors, and the full peacetime American governmental regime, nationally and locally. Indeed, at the political and military command level, the use of force and of the levers of commercial law and economic life also need to be considered together. In political terms, the effort to isolate the Cuban economy has become an extremely complex edifice of institutional arrangements at all levels of government, enforced in collaboration with the private sector. In military terms, it is true that an enemy can sometimes be denied access to satellite imagery by contract, rather than by taking out the satellite. Or that an ally can be disciplined by denying a license to re-export sensitive technology to a regime we do not view favorably. Or that private corporations can bring security to failed states, or be a force multiplier in conflict zones.

If you stay in a Hilton Hotel, you know that Mr. Hilton will not tuck you in—but you might well imagine you are staying in and being looked after by a unified corporate entity called "Hilton Hotels." This is quite unlikely—the functions of the hotel will undoubtedly have been unbundled and rearranged. One company may own the bars and restaurants; the housekeepers may be leased from a different service provider; risks to and entitlements from the income stream of the operation, as well as "ownership" of the building and its contents, will have been parceled out among all manner of financial interests by a combination of contract and property law arrangements. Businessmen and their corporate counsel are accustomed to working with a legal system that treats property as a series of discrete rights and privileges—to use, sell, rent, inhabit, and so forth—that can be arranged in a variety of ways. And they are used to designing legal entities whose authority can be also be arranged in various ways, splitting responsibility for decision making between shareholders, management, and employees, for example.

The public law structuring the military function in a modern state is of parallel complexity, and the unbundling of the "sovereign power to make war" into a range of public and private competences, shared out among many departments, opens a range of opportunities for military planners. Should it be the marines, the air force—or the CIA? Many departments of government will be involved, their responsibilities and powers parceled out by complex administrative arrangements. The military itself will be an amalgam of the various services and their component parts. There will be allies to coordinate, and, increasingly, a range of civilian and private partners.

The chain of command may be formally unified at the top, narrowing until the chairman of the Joint Chiefs advises the secretary of defense and the president. But we know that the networks of cooperation among their staffs and the broader political and administrative culture of Washington make a meeting of that type more symbolic than decisive. Those are the meetings they like to have photographed: the president consults his cabinet and decides. But when the chain of command is most unified, it also splays out into the broader political process. Members of Congress will have a say, as will defense contractors and insurance companies and the intelligence services and the president's political advisors. And there will be the informal pressure brought to bear up and down the chain by the media, by veterans groups, by the families of soldiers, and so forth. Military professionals looking ahead to that will take it into account, and build political and commercial concerns back into their military strategy. Political strategists will do the same.

Decisions about whom to allocate what responsibilities—or about the troop levels "needed to complete the job"—will reflect all these considerations and influences. A range of military and civilian rules, contracts, and administrative delegations will be the tools for implementing decisions about these matters. As a result, the strategy for battle is more than a schedule of things to shoot—it is also a plan to maintain support for the campaign, share risks and costs in a way that will be sustainable among objectives, and mobilize resources from the world at peace, and from the world of private commerce, into the public world of battle. In such a system, who does decide to make war, to kill these people? Who decides how many troops "we need" to deploy in Iraq? The president says he decides simply by listening to the military professionals on the ground. But do we believe him? Or is he saying that strategically? And what are they thinking—or saying—when they advise him?

It is not surprising that discussions of the Iraq war were filled with wild fantasies about who "really" was behind the whole thing—the neocons, Bush's obsession with his father, the exiles, Cheney, the Israelis, the oilmen—or simply the "hegemon," whoever that is. What we can be sure is that every Iraqi businessman who lost his livelihood during the occupation, whether to new competition or unstable electric supply or lack of security, will be able to develop an explanation if he wants to, of how his loss was rooted in American intention and strategy. Who is to blame for my son's death from cholera—Saddam Hussein, the Americans, the Shiites, the water supply board, the doctor?

In such a messy situation, law can also be an instrument for *attributing* responsibility. Let us imagine that you work for the military and have been tasked with a black operation to seize and transport suspects in the war on terror for interrogation in another country. Assume you have explicit authorization from someone who can trace their authority to the president. You are worried about whether this accords with the Geneva Conventions, but someone near the president's office has produced a legal memorandum interpreting the clear rules of the law in war to permit what you have been asked to do. It is not a prohibition—it is a privilege. You still need to develop the capacity to act. You need to put some kind of special secret agency together to do it. A few administrative authorizations, some statutory authorization, and there is the agency—you run it. You need funding—there will need to be an appropriation. Someone in the operation will report, at least in some way, to someone in the legislative branch. They might weigh in with secret memoranda raising concerns or suggesting things for you to consider. Some number of people will know about what you are doing, perhaps a few hundred by the time you get the job done.

There have to be dummy companies to pay people and buy things. Operatives will have to stay in hotels and somehow pay their room bills. They have to make phone calls. You might need to charter a plane to fly someone you capture off to the other country. The corporate forms and financial arrangements of the commercial world support your activity as they would that of any businessman, but you are also leaving a legal trail of contract and property and administrative practice. When your secret plane lands, the air traffic control people at the airport will routinely record the plane's serial number, written on the tail. The dummy companies might be legally registered, the bank accounts have to have signatories. An aggressive prosecutor, or an aggressive newspaper reporter—perhaps not in your country, perhaps somewhere else—might well pull the threads back together. Those in the legislature might get cold feet and make their memos public.

The institutional continuity of war and peace means that unraveling the secret war on terror is, in the end, not that different from unraveling a drug cartel, or the Enron scandal. You will need to foresee that this can happen, build this back into the planning stage. That might make you more insistent on secrecy, and take you further off the legal map. Or it might make you less ready to imagine that the only license you need will come from a lawyer reading the Geneva Conventions. Or it might make the lawyer analyzing the law in war engage in a far broader analysis of the context and a dynamic assessment of actions and their likely consequences. The embedded nature of the operation, and its potential for discovery, will influence the president's lawyer's assessment of the legality of the operation. And vice versa. However firm the international legal privilege to act may seem, he or she will need to take into account its disclosure, and its exposure not only to the formal jurisdiction of those with other views of the scope of the privilege, but of the persuasive effects of their arguments on the political and legal context for the operation.

Imagine that someone—a journalist, a foreign prosecutor, a legislative committee—starts unraveling these links and reconstructing who did what. As in any prosecution, there will be choices about how to attribute responsibility. These decisions will be shaped by legal standards of proof—whether someone acted reasonably, with intent, with knowledge, more probably than not, beyond a reasonable doubt—and by prosecutorial strategy. How should this person be charged, should we encourage them to cop a plea? The experience—our experience, the experience of those involved—of responsibility will be shaped by these standards and strategies.

We might say that responsibility becomes an effect of attribution, by others and by oneself. When the low-level guys cop a plea and implicate the big cheese, the big cheese becomes responsible. Unless or until this happens, he or she can remain safely "shocked" by what went down. Where the military may seek to isolate responsibility, humanitarians may seek to trace the chain of command, insisting that the buck stops with the broadest level of political or military responsibility. Law marks the links in the chain that lead to the president, or the secretary of defense, just as it separates the military professional from responsibility for the war's overall legitimacy. Interests that might otherwise find it difficult to ally with one another—private parties, governments with diverse ideological or cultural characters, differing religious groups—can find a common language of outrage in humanitarian law, as well as a readily available procedure for investigation and measure of responsibility.

To unscramble the tangle of mixed administrative responsibility for the abuse of prisoners is not only a matter of "getting to the bottom of it" or "finding out what happened." It is a cultural and political project of interpretation, which will often turn on and be debated in legal language. Sometimes it will make sense—to us, to someone else—to focus responsibility on this or that person, agency, ally. Sometimes it will be more sensible to spread it around. And there is no one person responsible for deciding which is the best way to go. People will have different ideas about that and will push and pull the retrospective analysis in various directions. Responsibility will, in the end, be the social effect of this process. But what kind of responsibility will this be? When the Democrats sense the chance to pin it on Rumsfeld, and Bush grabs the opportunity to highlight their unsuitability to assume responsibility for the nation's security, it is not at all clear we are any closer to the human experience of responsibility for having decided to kill all those people.

It would be odd if the political leadership did not treat the unraveling of these chains of responsibility as itself something to have a strategy about. It would also be odd if military commanders did not treat them strategically. Partly, of course, as an opportunity to send a message or reinforce the discipline of the troops. But also as part of the military's broader image and legitimacy. And also as a tactic of warfare. As a result, it would be surprising if those disciplined did not sometimes feel they had been "hung out to dry." Sometimes they will have been. They may be prosecuted or imprisoned to save face for the higher-ups. But they may also be imprisoned—as they may be sent to their death on the battlefield—as a tactic in the broader war, as a signal to the hearts and minds of allies or enemies or home front.

When turning questions of legitimacy into questions of responsibility can itself be a strategy, we will also want to think about the institutional and procedural possibilities. Who will decide whether it was the military, or the civilian authorities? Was it the Americans or the Iraqi police? Which branch, which private or public force, reporting to whom? In one sense, this will be decided by an open-ended social and political conversation about the legitimacy of action in war. But that is a bit vague. What about holding a congressional hearing, or setting up an independent commission, or ordering an investigation in house, or asking the United Nations to investigate, or . . . Of course all this will take some time. We will need to trace responsibility through the thicket of institutions and layers of "sovereign" authority exercised by different departments and agencies and powers, in the United States, in Iraq. Time is as important as territory in shaping strategy in war. So also in peace—assessing responsibility can change responsibility, just as it can legitimate or delegitimate an act. Passions will cool, circumstances may change.

Assessments of the legitimacy of battlefield action can now be parceled out in a process, as an inquiry into responsibility. But the days when the buck stopped anywhere are over—or, rather, stopping the buck is also a tactic. The photos are published, a flood of outrage, an inquiry—some bad apples are discovered, tried, punished. The media, the enemy, the Democrats push for more, inch their way through a complex chain of command. Before it gets too high, but when it already seems old news, the president steps forward and "takes full responsibility." Taking responsibility has become a rhetorical act—the continuation of politics by other means. But also an act of war.

The Abu Ghraib prisoner abuse broadly delegitimated the American military campaign in the eyes of many audiences. But it also focused those who opposed the war on violations and violators who could be identified and punished—on the bad apples. Once the Iraqi administration had taken over the prisons, it became easier to offload political responsibility for abuse on their shoulders. In some broad historical sense, perhaps, the Americans were responsible, or Saddam Hussein was responsible—but for that matter we could say it was colonialism or oil or whatever that was responsible.

It may be possible to identify the bad act precisely—torture of this person here, in this prison—and to assign responsibility to one administrative unit, perhaps to this guy, in this quasi-private militia reporting to this faction of the Iraqi provisional government, which has these powers and these responsibilities, and so forth. But it may also be possible to set in motion a broad ethical and legal discourse about the legitimacy of everyone until nothing can be pinned on anyone. And it is not clear that justice will be done, or seen to be done, either way. This is also what it means for warfare to have become civilized.

Strictly speaking, the decision to make war has never been the responsibility of the law of armed conflict. The law in war began with more modest ambitions: to distinguish the battlefield from the civilian world and reduce the savagery of combat. As such, it was primarily the domain of the military professional—and their humanitarian interlocutors. Civilian leadership means leaving questions about the legitimacy of the conflict—the decision to go to war in the first place—to a different, political domain. As the law of armed conflict has become a vernacular for evaluation of the legitimacy of warfare, however, it has merged with the law of war. And the calculations of military commanders have merged with those of the political leadership. Military professionals find themselves turning increasingly to the law of war—find themselves unable to assess the legitimacy of wartime violence without assessing the legitimacy of the war itself.

We might say that the law of war has become the law in war's destiny. Just as perceptions about the law in war now affect the legitimacy of the conflict as a whole, broad perceptions of the legitimacy of the war can affect how the laws in war are understood and applied. If the use of force is to be proportional—more force for more important objectives—it seems reasonable to think there would be a sliding scale for more and less important wars. Wars for national survival, wars to stop genocide—shouldn't they legitimate more than run-of-the-mill efforts to enforce UN resolutions?

We might think that collapsing the permissibility of tactics into the legitimacy of the war will force us to focus more directly on questions of overall responsibility. Indeed, those who argued that bombing the bourgeoisie supporting the Milošević regime would be legitimate and proportionate, did so in part to extend the principle of responsibility, established in the Nuremberg trials for the high political and military leaders who made aggressive war to the population more broadly—responsibilizing the citizens of a democratic state by bombing them.

Responsibility has taken on a new hue. Transposed from ethics to law, it becomes an attribute of office—of the citizen, the soldier, the statesman—and the basis for legitimate response. Indeed, we know you were responsible only when you bear the costs. We know you were liable, were under a duty, when you must pay the price. When, in this case, you have been legitimately targeted. It is not at all difficult to imagine a drone, flying over the desert, and a man deep in a basement in Virginia triggering his joystick, letting loose a missile to send the message that the man in the Jeep ranger was a member of Al Qaeda and Al Qaeda was responsible. They would be made to bear the price. You can run, but you can't hide—that's what we mean by responsibility. The vocabulary we use to make the political decision to go to war no longer differs in kind from that we use to fight it—or that we use to parse its legitimacy afterwards. Indeed, in the parsing of this war we begin to condition the battlefield for the next.

As a vocabulary of politics, the law of force can be a flexible strategic asset. Most famously, perhaps, the Americans who defended the military response to the discovery of missiles in Cuba called the operation a "quarantine." It was an invention— there was no available legal act called the "quarantine," and it took rapid strategic thinking to devise a set of precise rules of engagement to support the claim that intercepting Russian vessels was not an "act of war." The point was to communicate something about the act: it was serious, it would be forceful, but it was not intended to start a war. It was only intended to eliminate the disease. An on/off vocabulary of war *or* peace would have been less useful. Thinking of military options on a sliding scale, open to reimagination, provides a more nuanced strategic vocabulary for building and comparing options. The point was also to shift responsibility. We didn't start this thing. We didn't escalate it. We just quarantined the virus. But let's say it hadn't worked out, and the world had been blown up. Would that have been Khrushchev's "fault?" What about the lawyers who persuaded JFK that a "quarantine" was a plausible nonwar option? Of course, everyone sitting around the Oval Office that week felt the weight of history and responsibility and decision. And yet, as professionals, they were also parsing their respective expertise, and honoring Kennedy as he-who-bore-the-ultimate-burden.

In modern corporate and commercial law, all the available institutional forms or financial instruments and security instruments are not set out in some code, for lawyers and businessmen are constantly inventing new forms, new modes of investment, new ways to share and allocate risks. The modern law in war is also a work in progress, open to invention. And, as in the corporate world, the most effective use of this strategic environment will be made when military professionals work together with lawyers and political strategists. The earlier a corporate lawyer is brought into a deal, the more helpful he or she will be able to be in devising strategic alternatives and ensuring that legal arrangements track the business strategy. The same is true for military lawyers.

In the international world, we imagine this shared vocabulary of principles and policy judgment to operate through conversation. States, private actors, NGOs, national courts are participants in an ongoing conversation about the legitimacy of state behavior—legitimacy judged by their compatibility with UN Charter principles. Conversing before the court of world public opinion, statesmen not only assert their prerogatives, they also test and establish those prerogatives through action. Political assertions come armed with little packets of legal legitimacy, just as legal assertions carry a small backpack of political corroboration. As lawyers must harness enforcement to their norms, states must defend their prerogatives to keep them—must back up their assertions with action to maintain their credibility. A great many military campaigns have been undertaken for just this kind of credibility. Missiles become missives.

It was in this spirit that President Bush went to the United Nations to announce that *he* would enforce the Charter—and if he succeeded, and the Iraq regime were to change, democracy and freedom be released, the legitimacy deposit in his account would be a direct transfer from the UN. Of course, it was a risk, but the UN was also daring, and risking in resisting. When the UN withholds approval or refuses to participate, it may delegitimate the military campaign. Let us suppose it does not stop it—a determined coalition pushes ahead in the name of Charter principles. In the easy cases, the campaign succeeds, the UN has missed out. Or the campaign fails, the UN is vindicated.

As the occupation began, it became clear that the difficult case was now ours. The occupation was more difficult than anticipated, the postconflict/postwar/peacebuilding/nation-building phase held hostage the ultimate success or failure of the campaign. Op-ed writers urged all parties to ignore sunk costs, to focus on the future; surely we all have a stake in a successful outcome, and it makes sense for the United States and the international community to cooperate. Perhaps—but sunk costs cannot be ignored so readily. Seen dynamically, it made sense for Bush to resist relying on the UN to make good his original wager as precedent for the next case. Just as it made sense for the UN to resist engagement. It is no accident that we sometimes felt the Europeans *wanted* the project to fail. Sometimes they did, for in this game of meaning and precedent, to ignore sunk costs and get with the program is to take a legitimacy hit. Either way, Iraqi citizens—and American soldiers—paid the price, not in the "great game" of nineteenth-century diplomacy, but in the "great conversation" of twentieth-century legitimacy.

If, interpreting the law in war, humanitarians were loath to speak about the civilians who might legitimately be killed— "you just can't target civilians"—they also resisted the suggestion in the law of war that they, like military planners, decide when to draw down and when to pay into their legitimacy stockpile, and therefore, when to accept civilian casualties as necessary for longer-term objectives. Although humanitarians *talk* about the long-run benefits of building up the UN system or promoting the law of force, they do not make such long-run calculations. Current costs are discounted, future benefits promised—as if there were nothing to weigh *against* expansion of humanitarian institutions and ideas, no civilians who needed to be allowed to die for the legitimacy of the United Nations. But in this, we depart from pragmatic calculation altogether, into the domain of *absolute virtue*. We are back speaking truth to power. Civilians often think of humanitarians as gentle civilizers, lawyers whispering in the admiral's ear, protesters marching in the streets for peace, scholars documenting the norms and standards of humanitarian law, teachers instructing soldiers in the *limits* to warfare. Humanitarian rulership is often rulership denied. But it is not clear our military and political leadership is much better at grasping the gold ring of responsible decision.

Their strategic vocabulary has limits, blind spots, biases. In a sense, all the players have become role occupants. The president promises to "preserve, protect and defend the Constitution of the United States," by asserting the national interest on the global stages and defending the prerogatives of executive power. The military carries out his decisions. The humanitarian owes fealty to his norms and carries out the mandate of his institution. And so forth. Not all voices are heard, not all concerns calculated, by the group of elites we call "the international community." Humanitarians may focus too much on the United Nations as a proxy for world public opinion, or on the UN's involvement as a proxy for a humanitarian outcome. Everywhere, the abstractions we associate with the words "the national interest" will be treated as a legitimate basis for action. Doubtful as it seems, the Iraq war may turn out to have been in the U.S. national interest, if only because it took us down a peg. Perhaps the war was a bad thing for the international community, if only because it distracted attention from so many other serious problems—the quotidian injustices of "peace." But our normal political institutions and legal vernacular seem astonishingly ham-handed at focusing on determining these issues. Looking back, it is hard to conclude that opponents of the Iraq war were serious when they claimed their objection to the war was the lack of UN approval. Would the war really have made more sense to them had France had a different government? When great debates about war and peace are staged in the vocabulary of the Charter, a great deal is lost. The United Nations law of force makes the interpretation and operation of background rules, and the decisions of human actors, seem matters of fact rather than points of choice.

The Charter scheme encourages us to think of global policy as a combination of short multilateral police actions and humanitarian assistance. It distracts our attention from the economic side of the story—and from the development policy that comes with an invasion. It shortens our sense of how long—and how difficult—war to build nations or change regimes is likely to be. In the Iraq case, international law and the UN Charter focused our attention on weapons, which when not forthcoming, delegitimated the entire enterprise. International law urged us to respect Iraqi sovereignty, making it all too easy to think our intervention in Iraqi affairs began with the invasion and ended with the handover of the bundle of rights we have decided to call "sovereignty."

The vocabulary of the Charter can make it more difficult to address the motives for war and devise alternative policies. Let us take say the administration's hawks were right: suppose that after September 11 it was necessary to "change regimes" from eastern Turkey to western Pakistan. In the months before the war, the international community found it difficult to discuss regime change straightforwardly. Ideas about sovereignty, the limits of the Charter, core humanitarian commitments to the renunciation of empire—all placed regime change outside legitimate debate. Yet supposedly sovereign regimes are already entangled with one another. They struggle every day to change one another's regimes in all manner of legitimate ways. Why should this all become taboo when force is added to the mix, unless war is no longer, in fact, in Clausewitz's terms, "a continuation of political intercourse, with a mixture of other means."

When it comes to force, the Charter vocabulary offered an easy and irresponsible way out. We never needed to ask, *how should* the regimes in the Middle East—our regimes—be changed? Is Iraq the place to start? Is military intervention the way to do it? How do we compare various ways of combining military and nonmilitary "means" to the end of regime change? Had the Europeans not had the UN to shield them, not felt the geography of the European Union marked a legitimate boundary to their global responsibilities, they might well have drawn on their own experiences with "regime change," in Spain, Portugal, and Greece in the eighties, with the old East Germany in the nineties, and now with the ten new members states in central and eastern Europe. Why not EU membership for Turkey, for Morocco, for Jordan, Palestine, Israel, Egypt, regime change through the promise and example of social and economic inclusion rather than military force? Had our debates not been framed by the laws of war, we might well have found other solutions, escaped the limited choices of UN sanctions, humanitarian aid, and war, thought outside the box.

The modernization of the law of force was meant to enhance our ability to link decisions about the use of military force to the lexicon of political responsibility. That is what we mean when we applaud the transformation of law into a global vernacular of legitimacy. Unfortunately, however, this turn to language may have moved warfare further from the experience of political responsibility. Military and humanitarian professionals alike share the sense that somewhere else, outside or beyond their careful calculations, somebody *else* exercises political judgment and discretion.

Epilogue

Law and force flow into one another. We make war in the shadow of law, and law in the shadow of force. Law has infiltrated the decision to make war and crept into the conduct of warfare. We have bureaucratized and professionalized warfare—shifting responsibility always elsewhere in a war of the pentagon rather than a war of the spear. At the same time, the hand of force animates the world of law—enforcing its contracts, defending property, making its norms real in the world—making war on the enemies of the UN Charter. The boundary between war and peace—the contours of the battlespace—are marked and unmarked in the language of law, just as injury is privileged—and injurious conduct stigmatized—in legal terms. When Clausewitz spoke of war as the continuation of politics *by other means* he was confident the "grammar" of diplomatic notes and of artillery fire were distinctive. We have lost that confidence.

Clausewitz wrote brilliantly about the role of "friction" and "pause" in war—how myriad uncertainties and unexpected impediments unavoidably accompany warfare, and may leave both sides feeling it not to their advantage to attack outright. A common vocabulary of legitimacy, at once legal, ethical, and political, has become the friction—and lubricant— for war. Force has become a way of communicating, in a language at once of violence and political legitimacy. The pause in war has become the continuation of war by other means.

The etymology of this legal language shows traces of ethical debates about the justice of war, classical assumptions about sovereign prerogatives and the boundaries of war and peace, and an entire range of modern institutional and doctrinal efforts to render that language a pragmatic vehicle for statecraft. The changing practices of war and politics have also left their mark. The law of force today is a professional discourse of sharp distinctions and broad standards, of clear ethical judgment and nuanced pragmatic or instrumental assessment. It is also a lived practice, not something you can look up, or worry about only when you bump into its prohibitions. Whether the law will be firm or squishy, singular or plural, has become a matter of professional cultural reception. Warfare—like legal judgment—has become a social event. Claims and assertions, bombs and missiles, drop in a pond of social reaction. Prerogatives must be defended, defenses must be legitimate, and in this, war and law shake hands, reflect one another, remake and reinforce one another.

As a result, statesmen, military strategists, and humanitarians may disagree, but they are speaking the same language and playing the same game. Our military and humanitarian professions share in drawing and erasing the line between war and peace that once marked their respective domains. If ours has become a culture of violence, it is a shared culture, the product of military and humanitarian hands. If ours is history's most humane empire—if we are, in General Mattis's words, "humanitarian in all that we do"—that is also the collaborative achievement of humanitarian and military professionals.

Consequently, to resist war in the name of law, to exalt law as an external ethical restraint on the frequency and violence of war, to praise law for bringing the calculations of cool reason to the passions of warfare, is to misunderstand the delicate partnership of war and law. The laws of force provide the vocabulary not only for restraining the violence and incidence of war—but also for waging war and deciding to go to war. Although legal and military professionals may seem to march to different drummers, law no longer stands outside violence, silent or prohibitive. Law also permits injury, as it privileges, channels, structures, legitimates, and facilitates acts of war. We should be clear—this bold new vocabulary beats ploughshares into swords as often as the reverse. As a result, law has become a tool of strategy for soldiers, statesmen, and humanitarians alike. Law separates the wheat of just action from the chaff of aggression, wanton violence, or self-interest as an assertion, a tactic, or a strategy.

We may nevertheless hope that law could help identity the most important or promising opportunities for judgment and political contestation. But we should be wary of treating the legal issues as the focal points for our ethics and politics. Our fabric of norms focuses the attention of the world on this or that excess, while armoring the most heinous human suffering in legal privilege, redefining terrible injury as collateral damage, self-defense, proportionality, or necessity.

We may hope that law—whether a priori or ex post— might awaken our sense of responsibility for the terrible suffering of warfare. Sometimes this does happen. Someone may well prosecute this or that soldier, commander, or former president of the republic. But this activity also dissolves the broader experience of political and ethical responsibility, while assuring everyone else in the war machine—the voters and families and communities who sent their soldiers to battle, the commanders who directed them, the private firms who fed and supported and protected them, the politicians and strategic experts who thought the whole thing was a good idea, and the soldiers and pilots who slaughtered on the battlefield, that they were, in one or another way, not responsible for the suffering, foreseen and unforeseen, that resulted.

Statesmen who decide for war are adept at interpreting their decision as responsible—responsible defenses of their prerogatives, legitimate acts of authority, justified and necessary responses to the provocations of others, faithful implementation of a higher ethical purpose. When soldiers agonize, their chaplains, psychologists, and commanding officers reassure them that what they did was legitimate, justified, necessary. We support our troops, confident that they were privileged to kill, required to respond, honorable to serve, unable to resist, and that whatever violence they committed in our name was necessary and proportional.

But all these formulations, encouraged by the language of law, displace human responsibility for the death and suffering of war onto others—onto those who authorized the authority, those in whose name it is said to be exercised, those who will later hold office and be glad for the prerogatives preserved, those who define the higher ethical purpose, those who identified the legitimate military objective—or simply the enemy whose actions justified our response. In all these ways, we step back from the terrible responsibility and freedom that comes with the discretion to kill. In this, our political process has lost its moorings in responsible leadership, our democracy its potential for responsible citizenship and meaningful political contestation.

Indeed, in warfare today, we are better at assigning responsibility than experiencing it. We know that in war—as in all political life—you do not get what you bargain for. Unintended, apparently irrational consequences are the normal wages of military action. Unexpected suffering is everywhere to be expected. In the face of the irrationality of war, modern law has built an elaborate discourse of evasion, offering at once the experience of safe ethical distance and careful pragmatic assessment, while parceling out responsibility, attributing it, denying it—even sometimes embracing it—as a tactic of statecraft and war rather than as a personal experience of ethical jeopardy. Violence and injury have lost their author and their judge as soldiers, humanitarians, and statesmen have come to assess the legitimacy of violence in a common legal and bureaucratic vernacular.

The way out will not be to tinker with doctrines of the laws of force. If there is a way forward, it will require a new posture and professional sensibility among those who work in this common language. Recapturing the human experience of responsibility for the violence of war will require a professional style discouraged by the modern interpenetration of war and law.

For humanitarians, it will require abandoning the ethical self-confidence of normative denunciation as well as the pleasures that go with savvy participation in the instrumental calculations of proportional and necessary force. The problem for humanitarians is no longer an unwillingness to be *tough*—humanitarians have advocated all manner of tough and forceful action in the name of humanitarian pragmatism, and their words have legitimated still more. The problem is an unwillingness to do so *responsibly*—facing squarely the dark sides, risks, and costs of what they propose. Rather than fleeing from the exercise of responsible decision to the comfortable interpretive routines of their professional discourse, humanitarians should learn to embrace the exercise of power, acknowledge their participation in governance, cultivate the experience of professional discretion and the posture of ethically responsible personal freedom. International humanitarians, inside and outside the military, have sought power, but have not accepted responsibility. They have advocated and denounced, mobilized and killed, while remaining content that others governed and others decided.

The problem for military professionals is no longer a lack of humanitarian commitment. The military has built humanitarianism into its professional routines. The problem is loss of the human experience of responsible freedom and free decision—of discretion to kill and let live. For military officers and soldiers, renewing the experience of responsibility will require a reinvigorated sense of command responsibility, and an ethic across the force of refusing to allow the permissibility or privilege of force to lighten the decision to kill. This will mean a new kind of collaboration between legal and military professionals. The lawyer who carries the briefcase of rules and restrictions has long since been replaced by military lawyers who participate in discussions of strategy and tactics. As in many interdisciplinary discussions, it is easy for lawyers and other military officers to reassure one another in the terms of their respective expertise—"This is militarily necessary" and "This is just," they might say to one another. But cross-disciplinary conversations can also heighten everyone's experience of the limits of their collective professional vernacular, of the blind spots and biases of their respective expertise, and of their experience of human freedom. A better collaboration among lawyers and military strategists would bring the tools of each into question, and would focus the attention of each on the responsibilities of command and the human freedom of decision.

The most unsettling aspect of war today is the difficulty of locating a moment of responsible political freedom in the whole process by which war is conceived, waged, and remembered. Instead, we find humanitarians, military professionals, and statesmen speaking and being spoken by a common vocabulary of justification and excuse. To regain the experience of free political decision, we will need to awaken in all those who speak the language of war the human experience of deciding, exercising discretion, and being responsible for the results an unpredictable world serves up. For now, this experience is only available in those moments when the language of law dissolves and the professional presentation of the decision to kill as the legitimate and necessary unravels.

For all of us, recapturing a politics of war would mean feeling the weight and the lightness of killing or allowing to live. We must rekindle the sense that those who kill do "decide in the exception," to coin a phrase. As men and women, our military, political, and legal experts are, in fact, free—free from the comfortable ethical and pragmatic analytics of expertise, but not from responsibility for the havoc they unleash.

Most professionals flee from this experience—and their flight, their denial of both freedom and responsibility, accounts for their self-presentation as an expert, and increasingly, for their use of the vocabulary of the laws of force. But citizens flee from this experience as well. And they have also become adept in the language of war and law. We all yearn for the reassurance of an external judgment—by political leaders, clergy, lawyers, and others—that what they have gotten up to is, in fact an ethically responsible national politics. In a sense, the commander who offloads responsibility for warfare to the civilian leadership is no different than the foot soldier who cites failures of leadership, the lawyer who faults limitations in the rules, or the citizen who repeats what he heard on the evening news. Lay and professional, the languages of war, ethics, and law have become one. The challenge for all of us is to recapture the freedom and the responsibility of exercising discretion in this common tongue. Clausewitz was right—war is the continuation of political intercourse. When we make war, humanitarian and military professionals together, let us experience politics as our vocation and responsibility as our fate.

NOTES

Acknowledgments

1. Duncan Kennedy, "The Rise and Fall of Classical Legal Thought," 1975, unpublished.

2. Nathaniel Berman, "Privileging Combat? Contemporary Conflict and the Legal Construction of War," 43 *Columbia Journal of Transnational Law* 1 (2004).

Introduction: War Today

1. I am grateful to Charles Dunlap for alerting me to this phrase. See Charles Dunlap Jr., "Law and Military Interventions: Preserving Humanitarian Values in 21st Century Conflicts," Carr Center, Harvard University. Available at http://www.ksg.harvard.edu/cchrp/Web%20Working%20Papers/Use%20of%20Force/Dunlap2001.pdf; Charles Dunlap Jr., "Learning from Abu Ghraib: The Joint Commander and Force Discipline," *Proceedings* (U.S. Naval Institute), September 2005, 34–38.

1 ✛ War as a Legal Institution

1. John Jackson, William Davey, and Alan Sykes, eds., *Legal Problems of International Economic Relations: Cases, Materials, and Text on*

the National and International Regulation of Transnational Economic Relations, 4th ed. (St. Paul, Minn.: West, 2002), 1.

2. Wilhelm Röpke, "Economic Order and International Law," 86 *Recueil des cours* 223, 227 (1954).

3. James Carroll, *House of War: The Pentagon, a History of Unbridled Power* (Boston: Houghton Mifflin, 2006), 30.

4. Carl von Clausewitz, *On War*, ed. and trans. Michael Howard and Peter Paret (Princeton: Princeton University Press, 1976), 605.

5. Helmuth, Graf von Molke, *Moltke on the Art of War: Selected Writings*, ed. Daniel J. Hughes, trans. Daniel J. Hughes and Harry Bell (Novato, Calif.: Presidio Press, 1993), 124.

6. Clausewitz, *On War*, 76.

2 ✦ The Historical Context: How Did We Get Here?

1. For further analysis of their thought, see David Kennedy, "Primitive Legal Scholarship" 27 *Harvard International Law Journal* 1 (1986).

2. Francisco de Vitoria, *Francisci de Victoria De Indis et De ivre belli relectiones*, ed. Ernest Nys., trans. John Pawley Bate (Washington, D.C.: Carnegie Institution of Washington, 1917; reprint Buffalo, N.Y.: William S. Hein, 1995), 155.

3. Vattel, *The Law of Nations, or, Principles of the Law of Nature* (Northampton, Mass.: Printed by Thomas M. Pomroy for S. & E. Butler, 1805), v (spelling rendered contemporary).

4. Ibid., at 268–69.

5. Carl von Clausewitz, *On War* (1832), ed. Anatol Rapoport (Baltimore: Penguin, 1968), 402.

6. Henry Kissinger, *Nuclear Weapons and Foreign Policy*, abridged ed. (Garden City, N.Y.: Doubleday, 1958), 105.

7. "Lincoln at the Young Men's Lyceum in Springfield," 1838, in *The Complete Works of Abraham Lincoln*, ed. John G. Nicolay and John Hay (New York: Tandy, 1905), 1:35–50.

8. Kissinger, *Nuclear Weapons and Foreign Policy*, 105 n. 1.

9. Jonathan Zasloff has traced this influence among legal professionals participating in the formation of American foreign policy

from the late nineteenth century through the outbreak of World War II. See "Law and the Shaping of American Foreign Policy: From the Gilded Age to the New Era," *NYU Law Review*, April 2003, and Jonathan Zasloff, "Law and the Shaping of American Foreign Policy: The Twenty Years' Crisis," UCLA School of Law Research Paper No. 03-6, April 2003, available at http://ssrn.com/abstract=395962.

10. Quoted in Zasloff, "Law and the Shaping of American Foreign Policy: From the Gilded Age to the New Era," 47.

11. Raymond Aron, *Peace and War: A Theory of International Relations*, trans. Richard Howard and Annett Baker Fox (Garden City, N.Y.: Doubleday, 1966), at 374.

12. Nathaniel Berman has written a series of studies of this modernist interwar legal consciousness. See particularly "In the Wake of Empire," 14 *American University International Law Review* 1515 (1999) (First Annual Grotius Lecture, American Society of International Law); "Nationalism 'Good' and 'Bad': The Vicissitudes of an Obsession," 90 *Proceedings of the American Society for International Law* 214 (1996); "Economic Consequences, Nationalist Passions: Keynes, Crisis, Culture, and Policy," 10 *American University Journal of International Law and Policy* 619 (1995); "Between 'Alliance' and 'Localization': Nationalism and the New Oscillationism," 26 *NYU Journal of International Law and Policy* 901 (1994); " 'But the Alternative is Despair': European Nationalism and the Modernist Renewal of International Law," 106 *Harvard Law Review* 1792 (1993).

13. Harold Nicolson, *Diplomacy* (New York: Harcourt Brace, 1939), at 157.

14. Alfred Zimmern, *The League of Nations and the Rule of Law, 1918–1935*, 2nd ed. (London: Macmillan, 1939), 147. After 1945, Inis Claude described the lesson.

> [T]he conduct of the war had made a tangible contribution to the body of experience in creation and operation of multilateral agencies which was available to the founders of the League. Great Britain, France, and Italy, ultimately joined by the United States, had improvised an impressive network of joint bodies, including a

Supreme War Council, a Revictualling Commission, an Allied Maritime Transport Council, and a Blockade Council. These agencies had proved invaluable in facilitating the complicated task of fighting together. They had seemed to prove that effective international cooperation could be achieved, without the necessity of creating an authoritative decision-making body to issue orders to national governments, by bringing together responsible officials of governments to get to know and trust each other, to confront the full and true facts of the situation together, and to harmonize their national policies on the basis of respect for the facts, and appreciation of the positions of the various governments.

He found a similar relationship between the allied experience in the Second World War and the origins of the United Nations. Inis Claude, *Swords into Ploughshares: The Problems and Progress of International Organization*, 4th ed. (New York: Random House, 1971), 47.

15. Harold George Nicolson, *Peacemaking, 1919* (Gloucester, Mass.: P. Smith, 1984), 187.

16. Ibid., at 37.

17. Louis Henkin, *How Nations Behave: Law and Foreign Policy*, 2nd ed. (New York: Published for the Council on Foreign Relations by Columbia University Press, 1979), 137.

18. Oscar Schachter, "Dag Hammarskjold and the Relation of Law to Politics," 56 *American Journal of International Law* 1, 2, 4–5, 7 (1962).

19. See Oscar Schachter, "The Invisible College of International Lawyers," 72 *Northwestern University Law Review* 217 (1977).

20. My thanks to Ken Watkin for this example. See *Law of Armed Conflict at the Operational and Tactical Levels*, available at http://www.forces.gc.ca/jag/training/publications/law_of_armed_conflict/l oac_2004_e.pdf. The Canadian military manual states in chap. 17, par. 1702:

1. Common Article 3 to the 1949 Geneva Conventions and Additional Protocol II to the Geneva Conventions (AP II) are

the legal instruments dealing specifically with non-international armed conflicts.

2. Today a significant number of armed conflicts in which the CF may be involved are non-international in nature. As stated, the law applicable to such conflicts is limited. It is CF policy, however, that the CF will, as a minimum, apply the spirit and principles of the LOAC during all operations other than domestic operations.

21. For an analysis of this history, see Berman, "Privileging Combat?" 14ff.

22. Oliver Wendell Holmes Jr., "The Path of the Law," 10 *Harvard Law Review* 457, 461 (1897).

3 ✦ War by Law

1. For a terrific reinterpretation of the laws of war placing this "privilege to kill" at the center of the analysis, see Berman, "Privileging Combat?"

2. On the challenge of using riot control agents in an armed conflict setting, see Ken Watkin, "Controlling the Use of Force: A Role for Human Rights Norms in Contemporary Armed Conflict," 98 *American Journal of International Law* 1, 32 (2004), available at http://www.asil.org/ajil/watkin.pdf.

3. An excellent account of the relationship between this military decision and the legal culture that surrounded it is Michael Lewis, "Law of Aerial Bombardment in the 1991 Gulf War," 97 *American Journal of International Law* 481 (2003).

4. The unavoidable strategic use of law of war distinctions is best developed in Berman, "Privileging Combat?" Berman's analysis is particularly imaginative in its reinterpretation of the law in war from the perspective of the "privilege to kill."

5. Thom Shanker, "The Struggle for Iraq: Strategy; U.S. Prepares a Prolonged Drive to Suppress the Uprisings in Iraq," *New York Times*, April 11, 2004, Late Edition, Final, sec. 1, p. 1.

6. Quoted in Dexter Filkins, "A Nation at War: In the Field. Marines; Either Take a Shot or Take a Chance," *New York Times*, March 29, 2003, Late Edition, Final, sec. A, p. 1.

7. International Court of Justice, Case Concerning United States Diplomatic and Consular Staff in Tehran (United States of America v. Iran) Order of 15 December 1979, Provisional Measures, par. 3, p. 11.

8. International Court of Justice, Case Concerning Military and Paramilitary Activities in and against Nicaragua (Nicaragua v. United States of America) Order of May 1984, Request for the Indication of Provisional Measures, pars. 33–37, at pp. 183–85.

9. Figures all quoted in Carroll, *The House of War*, at 47–51.

INDEX